THE
HAPPY
HIGH
ACHIEVER

THE HAPPY HIGH ACHIEVER

8 ESSENTIALS TO OVERCOME ANXIETY, REDUCE STRESS AND ENERGIZE YOURSELF FOR SUCCESS

DR MARY E. ANDERSON

BLUEBIRD

First published 2024 by Hachette Book Group, Inc

First published in the UK 2024 by Bluebird
an imprint of Pan Macmillan
The Smithson, 6 Briset Street, London EC1M 5NR
EU representative: Macmillan Publishers Ireland Ltd, 1st Floor,
The Liffey Trust Centre, 117–126 Sheriff Street Upper,
Dublin 1, D01 YC43
Associated companies throughout the world
www.panmacmillan.com

ISBN 978-1-0350-5353-7

Copyright © Mary E. Anderson 2024

The right of Mary E. Anderson to be identified as the
author of this work has been asserted by her in accordance
with the Copyright, Designs and Patents Act 1988.

All rights reserved. No part of this publication may be reproduced,
stored in a retrieval system, or transmitted, in any form, or by any means
(electronic, mechanical, photocopying, recording or otherwise)
without the prior written permission of the publisher.

Pan Macmillan does not have any control over, or any responsibility for,
any author or third-party websites referred to in or on this book.

The information provided in this book is not an alternative to medical advice
from your doctor or other professional healthcare provider. You should not
delay in seeking medical advice, disregard medical advice or discontinue
any medical treatment because of the information provided in this book.

The individuals in this book represent composites of numerous patients
I have seen throughout the years. Their names and identifying information
have been disguised to an extent that any resemblance to any person, living or
dead, is purely coincidental. I have done this to protect patient privacy, while
maintaining the spirit and substance of the work.

1 3 5 7 9 8 6 4 2

A CIP catalogue record for this book is available from the British Library.

Print book interior design by Bart Dawson.

Printed and bound by CPI Group (UK) Ltd, Croydon, CR0 4YY

This book is sold subject to the condition that it shall not, by way of
trade or otherwise, be lent, hired out, or otherwise circulated without
the publisher's prior consent in any form of binding or cover other than
that in which it is published and without a similar condition including
this condition being imposed on the subsequent purchaser.

Visit **www.panmacmillan.com/bluebird** to read more about all our books
and to buy them. You will also find features, author interviews and
news of any author events, and you can sign up for e-newsletters
so that you're always first to hear about our new releases.

For my patients,
your courage and candor inspire me every day

CONTENTS

Introduction — xi

PART ONE
BUILD YOUR FOUNDATION FOR SUCCESS

Optimize Your Thoughts for Success — 3
Understanding the Troublesome Trifecta — 17

PART TWO
MEET THE 8 ESSENTIALS

Essential #1: Strive for Excellence, Not Perfection — 31
Essential #2: Invest in the Ultimate Currency: Your Energy — 57
Essential #3: Navigate Uncertainty with Curiosity — 83
Essential #4: Cultivate Healthy Connections — 105
Essential #5: Transform *Shoulds* to *Cans* — 131
Essential #6: Level Up to Gratitude-Based Thinking — 157
Essential #7: Celebrate the Victories — 179
Essential #8: Curate Meaningful Goals, Create Your Legacy—Start Now! — 201

PART THREE
KEEP MOVING FORWARD

Enjoying a Lifetime of Excellence — 219
Your 8 Essentials To-Go — 231

Acknowledgments — 239
Notes — 243
About the Author — 251

THE
HAPPY
HIGH
ACHIEVER

INTRODUCTION

I wrote this book for you. Yes, *you*.

If you're reading these pages, the odds are that you are an ambitious, hardworking person who is struggling with anxiety, stress, and exhaustion—even as you appear to excel.

And maybe, just maybe, it's not easy for you to pick up this book. Maybe asking for help is hard. Because you're someone who prides yourself on being self-sufficient no matter how heavy the burden, on charging ahead no matter the obstacle. Perhaps your instinct to disguise any imperfection, to present as unflappable, to please others in order to get ahead, is at war with your need for support.

I get that. I really do.

In fact, this pattern is typical of the people who so often find their way to my therapy couch—whether virtually or in person—allowing me the privilege of listening. Countless times, I've watched new patients drop their flawless facades (and tensed shoulders) once in my office, revealing themselves to be driven, determined, often brilliant, but also riddled with self-doubt, dread, and worry.

After years in the field, I have come to think of this phenomenon as high achiever's anxiety. And I see it as a kind of epidemic.

The bad news is that right now you are likely not feeling your best. You may be overwhelmed, tired, and frustrated by what feels like an insurmountable mountain of effort, and the truth is, if you continue on this track, you *will* burn out.

But you don't have to.

Though you may have imagined otherwise, I am here to tell you that your anxiety is *not* the price of admission for your success. You can feel better without losing your edge. In fact, if you feel better, you will thrive. You can be happy *and* high-achieving.

• • •

As soon as I began seeing patients early in my career, I observed this high achiever's phenomenon over and over again, too obvious to ignore. Almost every patient who walked through my door was burned out and unsure of how long they could sustain the pace of their relentless schedules and demands. They were plagued by feelings of inadequacy no matter how high they soared.

Sound familiar?

I recognized many of their qualities myself. After all, years ago, I overcame my own habit of people-pleasing.

Well over a decade of working with ambitious, anxious patients has concretized my understanding of high achievers' struggles and fueled my commitment to helping them find success and joy. When they first arrive, my clients are these awesome people who aren't yet enjoying their excellence. They're so bogged down with stress that they can't relish the fact that they're crushing it!

No more.

I am here for you, *with* you, and I have the expertise to help using science-based strategies I've formulated to combat the unique pressures and pitfalls of high-performing individuals—so you can flourish.

ARE YOU AN ANXIOUS HIGH ACHIEVER?

Among other things, high achievers are productive, talented, goal-oriented, skilled problem-solvers who love—I mean, *love*—a list. And these are advantageous traits! Maybe you recognize some of them in yourself. Or maybe some of these less enjoyable anxious high-achiever qualities also resonate:

- You are overwhelmed by self-doubt and your overextended schedule.
- You like to feel in control.
- You feel massive pressure to keep achieving big and impressive goals.
- You desire certainty.
- You experience fear of failure, of making mistakes, or of being viewed as incompetent.
- You're afraid others will find out that you're not as smart or talented as they thought you were.
- You are self-critical, often thinking about what you *should* have done or *should* do in the future.
- You worry about your performance and others' perceptions of your performance.
- You like to feel special instead of like "most people."
- You have tense muscles and often hold your breath.
- You suffer from difficulties with sleep.
- You have trouble saying no because of people-pleasing.
- You have unrealistic or perfectionist expectations for yourself, your family, your friends, and your coworkers.
- You see asking for help as weakness or failure.
- You get impatient or annoyed with things that feel unnecessarily long and prefer bite-size nuggets of wisdom that bottom-line the point quickly (like this list!).

If you recognize yourself in any of the above, if you love bullet points and hate saying no to your boss, if you think living at a frenzied pace with chronic stress and self-criticism is the necessary cost of success, you have found your way to the right book.

• • •

Raised to value hard work and service to others, I am passionate about helping as many people as possible. I earned my PhD in clinical psychology, specializing in health psychology, from the University of Florida, completed my internship and post doctoral fellowship at the VA Boston Healthcare System with appointments at Harvard Medical School and Boston University School of Medicine, then eventually became the chief of behavioral medicine at my group practice in Boston. I started working with high achievers organically, as the city is teeming with successful business and medical professionals, graduate students, and athletes who contend with chronic anxiety, intense worry, and imposter syndrome. During a later stint in California, I found that, despite a lot more sunshine, my high-achieving patients there suffered from the same challenges. Though some of my clients came to see the value of work-life balance over the course of the pandemic, they still felt—and continue to feel—inadequate and even more anxious and disconnected, sacrificing their health and happiness in order to prove themselves.

Fortunately, I have developed a cognitive behavioral therapy (CBT)–informed approach to help my patients navigate the particular challenges of high achievement. It's based around a concept I call the 8 Essentials, formulated with insights garnered from my clinical training, research in the field of psychology, direct work with patients, and expertise in CBT. The Essentials are practical principles to help you live well and optimally, free of the perpetual worry and overwhelm that can hold you back.

These tenets are game-changing in terms of guiding my clients to find relief, balance, and joy, helping them make better choices for their mental and physical health. With support, high achievers like you can shed self-doubt and continue to get ahead, without losing steam.

High achievers are action-oriented people who want concrete tools to take home and use. But after years of teaching these research-based strategies, I still couldn't find a text specifically tailored for high achievers, underlining the important concepts of the 8 Essentials in a concise and applicable way. So I decided to write one.

The foundation of my method is identifying how our thoughts, feelings, and behaviors are fundamental to achieving and sustaining our success and happiness. Once we understand that—including what I call the Troublesome Trifecta, or the three most persistent unhelpful ways of thinking that are obstacles to excellence for high achievers—we can begin the most important work: getting you relief as quickly as possible!

We need to combat counterproductive, energy-zapping habits that hinder your joy and, *yes*, achievement. Then, I'll give you the rocket fuel to accelerate your path to an excellent life. Plus you'll learn how to maintain those positive shifts and practices you've developed, so you can thrive without chronic anxiety for the rest of your life.

● ● ●

My psychologist friends and I often discuss how the people who wind up on our particular couches seem to arrive there for a reason. It's as if we were meant to work together, just like you were meant to pick up this book. You have arrived here for my help because you need it—and you are not alone. You've arrived here because you deserve to feel better.

If you're a high achiever, you probably hate to waste time. So let's get going. I'm excited for you because I have seen the incredible power of these Essentials in action: improving mood, sleep, relationships, and more. These changes in your cognitive and behavioral patterns will not only decrease your current anxiety but also proactively prevent such significantly elevated levels of anxiety and distress in the future, helping you achieve your goals.

So, picture yourself in my office, across from me on my comfy couch. You're letting your shoulders drop. You're breathing evenly. Your leg isn't bouncing. You've let the stress lapse for a moment, and guess what—you are still afloat. No one is thinking less of you.

You possess the capacity and power to optimize your life and become the best version of yourself. It is within your control to transform into a happy high achiever.

Now, let's do this!

THE HAPPY HIGH ACHIEVER

PART ONE

BUILD YOUR FOUNDATION FOR SUCCESS

OPTIMIZE YOUR THOUGHTS FOR SUCCESS

Your life is limited by the limits of your thoughts.
—Albert Einstein

Picture this: You're sitting in a meeting. It's not all-hands or make-or-break, but you and some of your colleagues and higher-ups have gathered around the big conference table or virtually, lattes and laptops at the ready. In the midst of some light brainstorming, you decide to share an idea. Your heart is racing, but this is your chance to shine! Only, before you can fully wow everyone, your boss stops you:

"No, actually, that problem was resolved yesterday," she says. "We're talking about something else."

No one seems to mind. Everyone moves on quickly. Everyone... except you. You want to disappear. Instead of moving past the gaffe, your mind spins into a shame spiral.

For the rest of the meeting and even the day (or week!), all you can think about is how deficient you were in that cringeworthy moment and, perhaps, are in life. You're consumed with how you sabotaged an opportunity to show your prowess. Maybe it's because you're not good enough? Maybe you're not working hard enough? Maybe everyone can now see your glaring imperfections, how you've been faking it all along?

Does that resonate?

My high-achieving clients come to me distraught over scenarios like this one all the time, stuck in overwhelming feelings of anxiety, shame, and imposter syndrome. As we start to talk, what we find is that it's very rarely the fumbled words or minor misstep itself that's standing in their way. Instead it's the unhelpful, anxiety-promoting thoughts that plague them in the aftermath that become the real hindrance to sustained success.

THOUGHTS, FEELINGS, AND BEHAVIORS— IT'S ALL INTERCONNECTED

The very first step on our journey—even before we meet the 8 Essentials—is to understand the powerful relationship between thoughts, feelings, and behaviors. These three elements—and how they affect each other—fundamentally shape how we experience the world.

Our *thoughts* (how we think about ourselves, others, and the world), *feelings* (our emotions, moods), and *behaviors* (our actions, choices, how we navigate the world) all directly impact each other. In fact, that interconnected relationship is so automatic to our functioning as humans that most of us have rarely, if ever, stopped to notice it:

```
            THOUGHTS
           ↗        ↖
          ↙          ↘
    FEELINGS  ⟷  BEHAVIORS
```

For instance, let's say you are *thinking* ahead to plans with a close friend and have the thought, "I can't wait to see Julie on Saturday!" You are likely to *feel* excited. If you're reading a good book on your couch (a cozy *behavior*), you'll *feel* content and relaxed. And have you ever noticed that if you arrive at work *feeling* happy and confident on a particular day, you're often more productive (a *behavioral* effect)?

Now, what if you're at a job interview for a position you really, really want and, as you shake the interviewer's hand, you *think*, "What if I freeze up?"—and then you *feel* extremely nervous? You may actually wind up *behaving* in a way that's disengaged, making minimal eye contact, and appearing less interested. Afterward, you might tell yourself, "See? I knew I'd mess this up!" And that *thought* only perpetuates the cycle of feeling stressed and anxious. But what if instead, as you shake the interviewer's hand, you *think* to yourself, "Wow, I'm so excited I got this interview! I'll do my best and no matter what happens, it's just really cool that I'm here!" Think about how different you would *feel* (probably motivated, proud, grateful) and how that would affect how you show up and *behave* at the interview (likely engaged, asking questions, and appearing curious, interested, and energetic). So, you can see how these three factors directly impact each other and how they profoundly impact your life. And that includes your professional activities and advancement.

We know that when people *feel* better, their *behaviors* are better, as well. In fact, research has shown that feeling happier will help you find more sustainable success. In Shawn Achor's internationally bestselling book *The Happiness Advantage*, he details his time at Harvard researching how "cultivating positive brains makes us more motivated, efficient, resilient, creative, and productive, which drives performance upward." As he notes, "This discovery has been confirmed by thousands of scientific studies and in my own work and research on 1,600 Harvard students and dozens of Fortune 500 companies worldwide."[1]

This is why, in CBT, an empirically supported treatment for anxiety and depression that is the basis for much of my work, we target improving both *thoughts* and *behaviors* to help people *feel* better. Feeling anxious, stressed, and insecure is unpleasant to say the least—and we want to release the pressure for you as quickly as possible. But it's important to note that our goal is not to eradicate our feelings completely. We need our emotions. Anger is there to show us a sense of injustice. Sadness demonstrates a sense of loss. Anxiety mobilizes us for potential upcoming challenges or dangers. That's why our goal is to modulate the intensity of our feelings, so they feel more manageable and we can more effectively move through them, rather than try to eliminate them.

That brings us to the main goal of *The Happy High Achiever*: to help you be both happy (*feeling*) and high-achieving (*behavior*). Your *thoughts* are going to be the key to making this objective a reality. And that's why they're going to come up again and again in this book. Thoughts are synonymous with self-talk. We are constantly in conversation with ourselves, whether we realize it or not. Unhelpful self-talk is going to make us feel bad and perform less well. Balanced self-talk is going to help us feel better and be our best. It's that simple.

THE POWER OF YOUR THOUGHTS

Now, before you panic, no, "self-talk" isn't code for overly earnest woo-woo affirmations! When I reference self-talk, I am referring to the thoughts that pass through your mind all the time that are fueling your feelings and impacting how you show up in the world. Self-talk can also be called your inner monologue or automatic thoughts.

Many of the wisest people in history, from Buddha to Marcus Aurelius to Maya Angelou, agree on the importance of our thoughts. As William James, widely considered the father of American psychology, said, "The greatest weapon against stress is our ability to choose one thought over another." And those choices around our thoughts are the foundation for how we move from anxious to happy high achievers.

So, thoughts can help us make great positive strides—when they're encouraging and not defeating.

In this particular book, you'll notice that I refer to helpful thoughts as "balanced" as opposed to "positive," which may be the term you're accustomed to hearing. This is not to diminish positive psychology, which is so important and intrinsically related to everything we're discussing. In fact, I'm an incredibly positive person, to the point where people have said my enthusiasm is like a "force" they can feel even over a Zoom call. But for my high achievers in the midst of anxiety spirals, positivity can also be a lot to ask. Saying, "Be positive!" to someone during a crisis can feel dismissive, to say the least.

That's why I often say, "I'm an optimist, but we have to stay real." There's a way to hold both. We can hope for the best while also staying grounded in the reality of a situation. What I'm trying to help you do is start finding *balance*. You don't have to like how you feel, but you deserve to know you're not alone and that there are tools to help you. So, while thinking positive may sometimes feel like too big of a reach, a balanced or helpful thought—a thought that *serves* you instead of detracting from your calm and confidence—can feel more accessible.

The bottom line: You can become a master of your mind. You can enhance your awareness of your thoughts, learn to transform your self-talk, and be your best.

Improve your thoughts, improve your life.

HOW YOUR THOUGHTS WORK

The first step to optimizing your thoughts is paying attention to them. Let's say you're back at work and, because you made that previous mistake at that earlier meeting, now you're nervous about contributing. You tell yourself, "What I have to say is probably dumb. People might think I'm amateurish if I say it."

How are you likely to feel after telling yourself that? Not good—right? More anxious, overwhelmed, and frustrated. And you could be more reluctant to speak up. So, one probable scenario is that you tell yourself, "It's just better if I don't say anything," and continue to feel stressed about talking at meetings. Not ideal.

This is an example of a cognitive distortion. Cognitive distortions are unhelpful thoughts originating from erroneous assumptions, misinterpretations, or maladaptive beliefs. Another version of that might be: "I said the wrong thing in a meeting and now everyone is going to think I'm bad at my job and I'll never get promoted."

If you didn't already guess, this manner of thinking seriously ramps up stress and anxiety, which makes everything harder. The thing about cognitive distortions is that all humans make them. A lot. Especially high achievers, who are prone to self-criticism and aggressively high standards.

Unhelpful thoughts lead to unhelpful feelings (distress) and unhelpful behaviors (not participating at meetings). They deplete your energy and keep you stuck, further reinforcing unhelpful/unbalanced thinking. It's a self-perpetuating, mood-sabotaging cycle. One we need to break.

This all sounds great in theory, right? You, like most of my patients, might be thinking: "Okay, Dr. A. But how?" Fair enough.

Our mission is to catch and conquer our cognitive distortions. Overcoming these ubiquitous beasts is not easy, but it's definitely doable. The first step is learning how to notice them. We have to get you really good at *knowing* when you are thinking a cognitive distortion (also sometimes referred to as "thinking errors" or what I'll call unbalanced or unhelpful thoughts). Then we move from awareness into action. When you recognize you are error-engaged, you can start challenging the heck out of it. And for that, you'll need your flashlight.

WHERE ARE YOU SHINING YOUR FLASHLIGHT?

So how do you recognize a cognitive distortion when it's happening? By how you *feel*. Thoughts impact feelings, which means you can work backward. This will be the easiest way to spot when you are thinking a cognitive distortion, because we don't often walk around saying, "What am I thinking right now?" but we do often know how we feel.

If you are feeling anxious, tense, on edge, nervous, or overwhelmed, ask yourself: What am I thinking? What am I telling myself right now? This is where you're shining your flashlight!

OPTIMIZE YOUR THOUGHTS FOR SUCCESS • 9

Your flashlight in this context is your attention. And where you aim your flashlight is just like choosing where you aim an actual flashlight in a room. You can choose to shine the beam right or left, up or down, and where the light is directed is what you'll see. The rest will fade into the background and stay in the dark. Similarly, if you choose to focus your attention on helpful, balanced thoughts or unhelpful, unbalanced thoughts, that's what you'll concentrate on—and that will impact how you feel.

If you're feeling anxiety, panic, or dread, most of the time you'll recognize you've been focusing on an unhelpful thought that is needlessly amplifying your anxiety. So, with the exception of traumatic situations that can naturally cause intense levels of emotions, if you're experiencing heightened levels of anxiety that feel unmanageable, then a cognitive distortion is likely the culprit.

When my patients are having particularly hard days, I'll ask them: "Where are you pointing your flashlight right now?" For high achievers, flashlights are often focused on their fears, self-doubts, and anxious thoughts about winning an upcoming case, landing a new role, earning the highest score, or submitting the best project. Or their attention is fixated on what others have accomplished—which, in turn, makes them feel inadequate.

TAKE ACTION

As soon as you can after your next stressful situation (so it's still easy to remember how you felt and what you were thinking), use the framework below to help identify the link between your thoughts about a situation and your reactions to it. What did you tell yourself during that situation? Where were you shining your flashlight? How did it make you feel and behave?

SITUATION ⟹ THOUGHTS ⟹ REACTIONS: FEELINGS & BEHAVIORS

Here's a sample version:

Situation: I want to ask a question in a meeting or a class.

Thoughts: This is probably a stupid question. People will think I'm incompetent if I ask.

Reactions:
Feelings—Anxious, nervous, insecure.

Behaviors—I don't ask the question and, thus, don't participate for fear of looking foolish. Someone else asks the same question and is rewarded with praise by the professor or higher-up.

Now you try filling out the info below!

Your Situation:

Your Thoughts:

Your Reactions:
Feelings—

Behaviors—

If you do this exercise regularly, you will begin to notice patterns and gain clarity about the situations in which unhelpful thoughts most often come up for you. And you'll start to see how your unhelpful self-talk negatively impacts your feelings and behaviors.

POKE HOLES IN DISTORTED THOUGHTS

Once you've shined your light on a distorted thought, the question is—how can you make that thought go away? (You're a bright person, I'm sure you've tried simply commanding a thought to leave and found that didn't work. That's why you're reading this book.) The good news is, while you can't make your thousands of thoughts stop or disappear, you can learn to poke holes in them, strategically helping yourself see where they don't make sense.

First, ask yourself: How is my thought *not necessarily* true? (You can likely list tons of reasons why you believe your thought *is* true. That's why the unhelpful thought exists in the first place.) Then, try to identify any aspects of your thought that are based on oversimplifications, inaccuracies, assumptions, or what happened in the past instead of what's happening now. We poke holes in our cognitive distortions by asking ourselves questions to find the evidence—the facts of the situation—that demonstrates our thoughts may be inaccurate.

For example, if your thought is about your mistake in the meeting, perhaps you can recognize that other people make mistakes in meetings all the time, so maybe your coworkers aren't likely to dwell on your small gaffe? Your boss told you you're doing a great job just last week, so maybe she won't decide you're inept because of one error?

When my patients who are law students express related anxiety about a mistake they made out loud in class, I often ask them, "When your classmates are speaking, are you really even paying close attention?" The answer is usually no. Let's be honest: Most of the time, people are focused on their own next thought, worry, or even phone and not on what someone else is saying. In fact, experts have identified a phenomenon called the "spotlight effect," or our "tendency to overestimate how much other people notice about us," and have found that people actually pay way less attention to what we are doing than we might imagine.[2] Most likely, your classmates aren't scrutinizing your every word, either.

Questioning the veracity of your unhelpful thoughts will help you overcome your current default, which is to automatically perceive all of your thoughts as truths. Why do our thoughts directly impact our feelings? Because we believe that our thoughts are *true*. If we don't treat our thoughts as facts, because now we know they are often based on cognitive distortions, they won't impact our feelings as intensely.

Think about a recent situation when you felt anxious. What were you thinking? When you identify which thought was the *most* anxiety-provoking and then poke some serious holes in that nasty overlord, your remaining unhelpful thoughts will be easier to conquer. Of course, this, like everything else, is a muscle that needs to be exercised so it can strengthen and become the new default.

Some additional helpful hole-poking questions to ask yourself:

- **Am I making this all-or-nothing?** Is there a gray area or middle ground to consider? Can I make a mistake, for example, without it meaning all is lost?
- **Am I making assumptions?** Am I trying to guess or predict what another person might think or what will happen in the future?
- **Are there other possibilities?** Could there be alternative interpretations or explanations about what happened?
- **Did I lose perspective?** Am I inflating the importance of something? Am I minimizing my strengths? Is this a life-or-death situation? If not, what are the actual consequences of this situation?
- **What might a trusted friend or mentor say about my thought?** How might someone else provide evidence to refute the accuracy of my unhelpful thought?

The good news: The more frequently you catch and poke holes in your cognitive distortions, the less power they'll have over you.

Continue to challenge them with questions and you'll begin to think more optimally and feel better!

NEW AND IMPROVED SELF-TALK—
WITH A TWIST OF HOPE

Once you've poked holes in your unhelpful thought, you can use the evidence you amassed to generate some new and improved self-talk. Here's the formula: A helpful thought pays homage to the reality of the situation and then gets balanced out, after an important "but," by what I call the Twist of Hope at the end. The twist is created from the facts you learned when you poked holes in the initial thought—that's why we call new and improved self-talk *evidence-based thinking*.

> **Pro Tip:** Make it believable and keep it short.

Let's look at an example: My patient Tina, an architect in her early thirties, came to our session feeling overwhelmed and burdened with worry about giving a presentation. Her boss had asked her that day to speak at the company's upcoming board meeting. "I can't do it, Dr. A," she lamented. "I'm going to mess up. Everyone will see how nervous I am. I'm not a good public speaker. I should be better at this." We talked through her concerns a bit and recognized that she was feeling especially stressed because she was focusing her flashlight's beam on her most anxiety-inducing thought: "I can't do it."

Can you sense the dread? Poor Tina felt terrified.

So we started poking holes in that sucker by asking questions. I asked, "How is your thought *not necessarily* true? You said you can't do it. Have you *ever* presented at a meeting before?"

In fact, she had. "Well, I spoke at the company meeting last year to discuss part of an important project I was point on," she acknowledged.

"Did you get negative feedback after that meeting?" I asked.

Tina shook her head. "No, my boss actually said I did a good job, and one of my colleagues told me it was helpful. But I don't like speaking at meetings and I don't want to do it. I'm so stressed out!"

So we crafted a more balanced thought for Tina: "I feel anxious about this presentation and I really don't want to do it, *but* I've done presentations before and even received some positive feedback. I'll prepare, practice a lot, and do my best to get through this one, too."

Notice we didn't encourage Tina to tell herself, "I like speaking at meetings. Everything will go perfectly." That Pollyanna sentiment wouldn't actually help Tina feel less anxious. Why? Our thoughts impact our feelings because we *believe* them. You're a savvy high achiever with a great brain! You're not simply going to accept a new thought because it sounds nice. Your new and improved self-talk needs to be *believable*—or else it won't help you feel better.

Additionally, an ideal balanced thought is also *short*—so it'll stick. Stick in your mind when it races with worry. Stick in your head when you're confronted with a sudden, stressful situation like an impromptu call from your higher-up or a deadline that gets bumped up a day. We know from the way our minds swarm with and glom on to unhelpful thoughts that they're often cruelly concise creatures that replay in our heads. Maybe some of these sound familiar?

I can't handle this.
What was I thinking?
I'm not good enough.
They'll see right through me.
It won't work.
What if I fail?
This is too much.

A short, memorable phrase will help you combat those crafty, malevolent ones. So try to shorten your new and improved self-talk to the least number of words possible. Tina decided this abbreviated balanced thought worked best for her: "I don't like giving presentations, but I've done this well before." She practiced it whenever her unhelpful thoughts about the meeting started creeping back into her self-talk. Tina also posted a brightly colored sticky note at the bottom of her computer that read I'VE DONE THIS BEFORE to keep her moving forward as she prepared and practiced her PowerPoint presentation. And when the meeting day arrived, she was ready for it.

I encourage my patients to choose whichever words feel most true and most effective in assuaging their anxiety. No one knows what resonates with you as well as you do! With that in mind, here are some conveniently compact, constructive self-talk phrases you can try out. Use them as-is or to jump-start your own new balanced thoughts. Ask yourself: What feels most believable?

- *I got this.*
- *I can handle this.*
- *I'll get through this.*
- *I'm not alone.*
- *I can't control everything.*
- *I'll do my best.*
- *I can go and see what happens.*
- *This isn't life-or-death.*

In the spirit of embracing reality, it's also important to accept that, though it can be uncomfortable, some level of anxiety is normal. In fact, anxiety is essential to alerting us to potential dangers. The problem is that high achievers are almost preternaturally gifted at thinking ahead to potential scenarios. For instance, my lawyer clients can anticipate possible counterarguments and maneuvers by opposing counsel, which is helpful in their careers—but that can become problematic when applied to their personal lives. So you see the issue: Your tendency to analyze, recognize the inherent uncertainties of life, and push yourself to accomplish great goals can also exacerbate your stress.

Anxiety may pop up at times, but you're working to equip yourself with the tools to help it feel less overwhelming. The more you practice your new and improved self-talk, the less frequent and more conquerable your old, unbalanced thoughts will become.

So, identify your most anxiety-provoking thought, poke holes in it by asking questions—and collect your evidence, and then create a believable-and-short balanced thought to shine your flashlight on instead. When your attention inevitably shifts to an unhelpful thought (and it will—because you're human), keep refocusing on balanced thoughts that help your emotions feel manageable. Remember: You're holding the flashlight. And balanced thoughts will energize you and keep you moving forward toward successfully achieving your goals.

Now that you understand the power of your thoughts—and you possess the strategies to overcome cognitive distortions—we can take the next step forward. Let's take a look at the three distortions that most frequently plague high achievers, so you can stay watchful for what you'll need to conquer to feel happier, be your best, and really crush it. And then the 8 Essentials await!

UNDERSTANDING THE TROUBLESOME TRIFECTA

If you correct your mind, the rest of your life will fall into place.

—Lao Tzu

We've already established that you love a list. (*That's right! I see you!*) Which is why, when an anxious high achiever settles in across from me in my office, sizing up my behemoth water bottle and fiddling with their shirt cuff, it's my practice to hand them a list of various cognitive errors.

Now, I know the word "error" might be freaking you out as a high achiever, but try to remember that everyone, I mean *everyone*, engages in distortions like these every day. They're ubiquitous, part of how our brains work, so let's normalize them. The problem isn't that we have them, it's that we don't catch them or challenge them.

My version of this list of distortions—which is adapted from the work of psychiatrist David D. Burns, MD[1]—is a kind of choose your own adventure of unhelpful, but deeply human, distorted thoughts. Thoughts that we *all* have sometimes, ranging from "Emotional Reasoning" (assuming that your emotions must reflect the truth or a fact—for example, if you feel nervous about getting on an elevator, you assume it means that elevators aren't safe) to "Discounting the Positive" (rejecting positive experiences as if they don't count—for instance, if you got published in an important magazine but dismissed the success because the article was "only" published online or because the editor made some changes). But when I ask my stressed-out high achievers to look through the list and identify what resonates, three specific cognitive distortions come up so often that I have come to call them the Troublesome Trifecta. (Cue the ominous music!) They are:

1. All-or-Nothing Thinking
2. Jumping to Conclusions
3. Should Statements

Together, this Troublesome Trifecta needlessly amplifies anxiety, drains your energy, and makes it harder for you to achieve your lofty goals. They are, in short, the constant hurdles on the path to success and happiness. As always, the first step toward diffusing these problematic ways of thinking—catching and conquering them—is identifying them and how they show up within what I call the Three Pillars of Life: home, health, and work.

ASK DR. A

Question: Can I stop myself from ever having cognitive distortions?

Dr. A: As a human, you're going to have unhelpful thoughts. And that's okay. It doesn't mean you're failing. So no, you can't stop yourself from having them altogether. But you can learn to respond to them more effectively. Thanks to neuroplasticity–our brain's awesome ability to change and adapt[2]–with repeated practice of more helpful self-talk, you are strengthening neural connections for healthier thinking. That means by poking holes in your cognitive distortions and practicing new and improved self-talk, you're creating new superhighways in your brain. Eventually, those will become your default. Your old, unhelpful ways of thinking will become like grassed-over country roads, no longer traveled. So the good news is that the frequency of those unhelpful types of thoughts will likely decrease over time the more you practice new, healthy self-talk. And even when those unhelpful, anxiety-promoting thoughts do pop into your mind, you'll know how to optimally respond to them so you can accelerate forward.

ALL-OR-NOTHING THINKING

All-or-Nothing Thinking—or what I also like to call Pressure-Cooker Thinking because it creates a crushing tension—is just what it sounds like: thinking in absolutes. This means seeing life only in rigid dichotomies: right and wrong, good and bad, perfect or a total failure. Everything is black and white. One of the first times I remember encountering this issue in my office was with a client of mine named Josh. He was an ambitious and energetic recent MBA graduate in his late twenties, clearly poised to do great things. But despite his trim haircut and tailored button-downs, which made him appear polished from an outside perspective, he was privately riddled with self-doubt. Like many of my high-achieving patients, he described feeling overwhelmed by job stress and, particularly, a specific project on which he was working. But when he talked about it, he didn't say, *I just want to do a good job!* or *I'm going to work my hardest, so I know I did my best.* Instead he said things like, "I want everyone to be completely blown away by my work."

As a high achiever yourself, you may be thinking, "So? What's wrong with that?"

Sure. Fair enough. Who doesn't want to wow their colleagues and bosses?

The problem arises when being the absolute best is the only acceptable metric for success, when—instead of simply wanting to impress your higher-ups with a job well done—you feel you must bowl them over with nothing short of perfection. Anything else equals failure.

Sound familiar?

Having high standards for yourself is great, except when they're taken to unhealthy, unrealistic, and even impossible extremes. Then they're at the heart of destructive perfectionism, unnecessarily turning up the heat on situations and setting you up for unhelpful thoughts and feelings, including:

- Anxiety
- Worry
- Self-doubt
- Overwhelm
- Disappointment
- Exhaustion

Why, for example, should someone like Josh, still early in his career, know how to perfectly orchestrate a type of project he had never completed before? That's a dangerous expectation on multiple levels. First of all, it leaves little space for innovation. The minute you begin evaluating and judging, the space for creativity narrows.[3] When you're self-conscious, it creates a rigidity that doesn't allow you room to explore and iterate. And openness is necessary for achieving excellence.[4]

Second, this idea that everything must be the best or worst, that achievements don't count unless they're flawless and at the pinnacle of what's possible, actually hampers your trajectory toward success. Having set themselves up for almost sure failure with unrealistic expectations, high achievers often become so afraid of appearing inept that they stop trying at all. Unmeetable standards can spur a kind of perfectionist paralysis or, at the very least, procrastination, which translates to wasted time. Clients like Josh might spend an excessive amount of time editing and re-editing an email and overthinking, for example, for fear of making a single mistake.

Third, working such long hours is not only unhealthy but also leads to burnout. I don't need to tell you how much less clarity you have after countless hours burning the midnight oil without breaks. You're a high achiever! You've no doubt experienced the toll firsthand. It leaves us fried, unlikely to interact well with others, accomplish tasks, or actually enjoy our lives.

And the emotional toll of walking around anxious and feeling like a failure all the time? Of perpetuating a cycle of self-doubt and disappointment? Of feeling exhausted and overwhelmed trying to do *everything* all the time? That's not just a miserable way to walk through this world. It's also not sustainable. Eventually, we all hit a wall.

This issue rears its head in multiple areas of life:

At home, in your personal life, perhaps you want to throw a party for a significant other and will not rest unless it's the Celebration of the Century, inspiring guests to heap praise upon you and then talk about it for years to come. It's not enough to throw a fun get-together.

When it comes to your health, maybe you set an expectation of hard-core HIIT workouts seven days a week. If taking even one day off feels like failing, then if you're injured or sick and your perfect record is ruined, you're likely to scrap the exercise (never mind other self-care) altogether instead of pausing and beginning again. Or perhaps you'll exercise anyway and push your body too hard.

In the workplace, that All-or-Nothing Thinking is likely to make you feel defeated in advance. Whether you're a lawyer prepping for a big trial, a student in the days before an exam, or a marketing professional readying for a pitch, your obsession with being the absolute best may actually trigger procrastination. And nobody wants that.

When you find yourself thinking things are either amazing or awful, the best or the worst, always or never, you're likely practicing All-or-Nothing Thinking.

TAKE ACTION

As you go throughout your day, try to catch yourself using these buzzwords:

- Always/Never
- Everyone/No One
- Everything/Nothing
- Absolute/Absolutely
- Complete/Completely
- Ruined
- Can't
- Perfect
- Failure
- Loser
- All
- Total/Totally

I often hear patients talking about how they're so "behind"—even at twenty-five years old! They think they need to be partnering up, buying homes, penning first-author publications, or winning higher titles. If they aren't the very best, what's the point? As high achievers, we are conditioned to strive to be the best in order to feel valued and lovable, and our culture can inadvertently exacerbate the issue. The expectations set up by movements like #GirlBoss are meant to empower, but often they ratchet up the heat on the pressure cooker. Additionally, the fact that we are *always* available and plugged in via our cell phones can feel like convenience, when it actually hinders our productivity because it burns us out. And then we wind up living with chronic anxiety.

JUMPING TO CONCLUSIONS

Picture yourself seated across from an old-school fortune teller as if in a hokey movie. The light is dim. Beads hang in the doorway. An intoxicating incense permeates.

"What do you see in my future?" you ask.

The madam squints as she peers into her cloudy crystal ball. "You will never get promoted, you will never find love, and your cholesterol will be very high. Also"—she continues, looking up to meet your eyes—"I'm judging you for being here. Why are you relying on a psychic for a life plan?"

Would you return to this shop? Would you trust the madam's vision? Probably not. And yet this is so often how we speak to ourselves.

Jumping to Conclusions, the second of the Troublesome Trifecta, is just as it sounds. It's the practice of making negative predictions about what might happen or what someone else is thinking and is often an unhelpful way of coping with uncertainty. This cognitive distortion can be broken down into two subtypes:

Negative Fortune-Telling: When you believe something in the future won't go well, even though it hasn't happened yet.
Mind Reading: When you assume that a person or group of people don't like you or are responding negatively to you, even though there is nothing confirming that fact.

Jumping to Conclusions is problematic because focusing on the future, especially on factors that we can't yet (or ever) control, can be detrimental not only to our happiness but also to our path to success. Often I have patients who sit across from me, wringing their hands and insisting that they'll fail the bar exam, that a date will be a disaster, that a presentation is doomed to flop. I can't begin to count the number of clients who, with real worry in their eyes, express dread about aging—when they're only in their *twenties*!

Of course, it's quite common to get bogged down in worries about the future. Especially for high achievers, who crave certainty and control, sitting with ambiguity and the potential for failure and disappointment is incredibly uncomfortable. The truth is that life rarely goes exactly as we expect, so trying to protect ourselves by predicting negative outcomes in advance is counterproductive, especially because we're often wrestling with issues that will never actually arise. More often than not, the real concerns that emerge are not what we stressed about anyway, so Negative Fortune-Telling becomes a waste of time and energy.

I understand this not only because of how often I see this phenomenon with my clients but also because I myself have fallen victim to it! For years, a little voice saying, "What if people don't like it?" stopped me from writing this book. What if it wasn't good enough? In the recesses of my mind, I imagined that the project—and I—would fall short, even when I knew I had the professional expertise.

Negative Fortune-Telling can be enough to stop you in your tracks. *Damn that crystal ball!* Take my patient Laura, who really wanted to find a life partner. When talking about an upcoming date, she sighed heavily and said, "I know it'll be just like the other dates I've been on, Dr. A. It'll be awkward, we won't click, and I'll just be sitting there waiting for the date to end." Her Negative Fortune-Telling caused her to feel anxious and even dread going on dates. And it really lowered her motivation to meet new people or check out dating apps, even though that's what would ultimately help her achieve her major life goal of finding a significant other.

This type of Jumping to Conclusions also drains us because worry is exhausting and distracting. It's hard to concentrate on accomplishing a task and doing your best in the present moment while you're shining your flashlight on worries about the future—what could go wrong or not work out well, negative outcomes of things that are important to you. If you've ever tried to work while worrying about bills or a conflict at home, awaiting a call from your doctor about test results, or checking your phone for a text from that person you're crushing on, you know it's super hard to concentrate.

So, Jumping to Conclusions actually hinders your ability to achieve success. One thing that helped *me* overcome this was that my goal of helping as many people as possible superseded my fear about what the future might hold. Focusing on my "why" is what gave me the courage to take action, sit down to do the work, and finish this book despite my initial negative forecasting. And I realized we earn courage by doing the things we are scared to do.

But what is it that makes us afraid in the first place? Often it's about our fear of not meeting other people's expectations. I know one of my worries was, "What if people think less of me?" Caring a lot about what other people think and the outside world's perception of you is a hallmark of high achievers. This is often at its most extreme when you really care how someone thinks or feels about you, and your fear of rejection overtakes your ability to think analytically. So in romantic situations, in job interviews, during meetings with your manager (or anyone else whose opinion you value), you're more likely to engage in inaccurate thinking and unhelpful self-talk.

Unfortunately, seeking outside validation is a recipe for anxiety and insecurity. And this is where Mind Reading comes into play. As much as we'd like to, we can't know what others are thinking in any given moment. And yet we assume that people are judging and reacting negatively to us when, frequently, we're just judging ourselves. How often have you assumed that a person or group of people didn't like you, only to find out later that they thought you didn't like them? Or that they hadn't yet formed an opinion about you at all? This cognitive distortion gets in the way of you building important relationships, both personally and professionally. Plus you sit around feeling bad about something that potentially isn't even an issue.

The reality is that worrying is the opposite of problem-solving. Jumping to Conclusions doesn't actually move us forward. Rather, we're running in a loop. Not only does it needlessly drain our energy, but it can become a self-fulfilling prophecy. If you think the HR person at a job interview doesn't like you, you may behave in a way that's less engaged, and thus maybe they won't. (Once again, your thoughts will impact your feelings and your behaviors.) If you think you're going to fail a test and have become really overwhelmed to the point where you procrastinated and didn't study, maybe you won't perform as well as you hoped. Jumping to Conclusions is like living life with a perpetual case of the "Sunday Scaries." And no one wants that!

SHOULD STATEMENTS

You probably feel like you *should* read this paragraph. You probably think others have done it before you—and faster! You probably think you should work on your anxiety. But my hope, instead, is that you'll read this because you want to and deserve to feel better.

Therein lies the complicated nuance of should-ing yourself, which is essentially when you pressure and beat yourself up about something that you think you should or ought to be doing because perhaps others are doing it or you feel you haven't ascended as high as you could (or should).

For high achievers, who notoriously set unrealistic standards, Should Statements (also referred to as "should-ing") are an unfortunate staple. My patients are often afraid to stop being hard on themselves for fear of becoming lazy or complacent, losing their edge. You know the drill: We tell ourselves we should be more successful, we should go to the gym every day, we should apply for that job that we don't actually want because the title and the company are prestigious and we're supposed to want that, right? It's all about rising as high as possible, even if that doesn't bring us fulfillment or meaning. Unfortunately, these constant shoulds are detrimental not only to our happiness and peace of mind but also to our forward motion.

When we should ourselves, we get stuck. This mindset makes us feel defeated, sparks self-criticism, and steals our sense of agency, so we're less motivated to take action to improve. At home, we might think, "I should maintain a perfectly organized space"—but faced with that expectation, we give up and simply feel less-than. When it comes to our health, we might think we should eat more kale, be skinnier, or look younger or more like someone else. At school or work, we think we should be acing every assignment and handling an intense workload without help, at all times. This can make us feel anxious, guilty, and insecure. (How's that for another trifecta?) In reality, a goal based on a should is not likely to be met.

And when we're in that should-ing zone, we are often not just should-ing ourselves. We also should other people. Through the lens of our unmeetable standards, we shine our flashlight on *their* perceived shortcomings. We feel they ought to be performing better, too, whether it's our romantic partner, coworkers, or friends. I always remind my patients that people have the right to be whoever they are, as long as they're not hurting anyone. But as high achievers, we often have strong opinions about how things "need" to be done and how others ought to behave. For example, I frequently hear clients express frustration about other people's inefficiencies around everything from their office's administration to the "incorrect" way their roommate or significant other loads the dishwasher to the lackluster service at their local café. Still, sitting and stewing doesn't get anything done either. Should-ing others can make us feel stressed, frustrated, or resentful.

Perhaps most significantly, because our shoulds are distorted thinking, they paradoxically make us more likely to *avoid* addressing whatever it is we wish was different—be it an aspect of ourselves, others, or a situation—and prevent us from effectively setting and achieving goals.

We wind up focusing more on what's wrong than on how to address the issue. Because when our *thoughts* are fixated on what's wrong, it makes us *feel* bad, guilty, and less motivated, and negatively impacts our *behaviors*, as well. So we aren't empowered to take action to improve our habits.

CATCH THEM IF YOU CAN

Sometimes I witness anxious high achievers embodying the Troublesome Trifecta all at once. (That's the kind of overachieving that doesn't help you!) "I should be able to handle all of this," they say, "or everyone will think I'm a failure." In those moments, I feel like I can actually see the weight they are carrying on their shoulders. I want to tell them to unload and leave all that heavy, unhelpful pressure in the corner.

Now that you've raised your awareness about when you're engaging in All-or-Nothing Thinking, Jumping to Conclusions, and Should Statements, you'll be prepared to take action and shed the burden of anxiety and stress as we step into the 8 Essentials in Part Two.

And remember: When you do catch your cognitive distortions, give yourself credit instead of beating yourself up! These are slippery little buggers! It's awesome that you caught them.

This is when we begin discussing how to defeat these distortions with specifically tailored strategies. We don't like to waste time, so let's dive in!

PART TWO

MEET THE 8 ESSENTIALS

ESSENTIAL #1

STRIVE FOR EXCELLENCE, NOT PERFECTION

*A flower does not think of competing with
the flower next to it. It just blooms.*

—Zen Shin

Imagine you're working on a project for which you have a very particular vision. But every time you put pen to paper, your execution falls short of your ideal. There's a gap between the perfect image in your mind and your ability to realize the concept in the moment. The more attempts you make, the more frustrated you become, until finally you crumple up one last sheet of paper, toss it in the trash, and storm away, giving up altogether.

Does that scenario resonate, either literally or figuratively? Perhaps you have memories of those kinds of classic anxious high-achieving frustrations even dating back to childhood. How many balled-up pieces of paper have you left in your wake while you walked away feeling defeated, like you failed?

This is perfectionism in a nutshell: the belief that everything you do has to be the very best or it's not good enough. In fact, unless it's flawless, it doesn't even count and isn't worth doing at all. What's troubling is that, when we set such unattainable standards, we lose momentum and lose trust not only in our endeavors but also in ourselves. The problem is not the drive to succeed, achieve our goals, or continually become our best self. The problem is that we tie our self-worth to our achievements, so we become terrified to make mistakes or ever look less than the best. Translation: We may believe that if we're not perfect, we're worthless.

So how do you know if you're plagued by anxiety-promoting perfectionism or are simply overwhelmed by too much on your plate? First, ask yourself: Is my stress and worry tied to how I think about myself? Shine your flashlight on your self-talk. Do you find yourself thinking, "I have so much to do! How will I get it all done?" Or are you telling yourself, "I should be able to handle all of this. I must really suck. What's wrong with me?" If you're primarily focused on the sheer volume of work, but you know your inherent value as a person is not contingent on whether you get it done, then you're likely just overextended. But if you are barraging yourself with self-criticism and feeling shame or inadequacy about your work, that's indicative of unhealthy perfectionism.

Perfectionism doesn't always manifest in all areas of your life. Frequently, high achievers are consumed with the parts that win them the most potential approval and are external-facing—appearance, achievement, relationships. For example, I had one hardworking client, Liz, who had chronic toothaches because she didn't prioritize going to the dentist on schedule, but she never missed her monthly hair appointment.

Now, there's nothing wrong with lofty goals or wanting to look your best. But the reality is that while striving for flawlessness has brought you some success in the past, it has cost you something, too. Those perfectionist tendencies aren't serving you anymore. You are probably feeling anxious, overburdened, and bad about yourself, and maybe you haven't been hitting your marks as much as you want lately, either. Because perfectionism is actually counterproductive. You may achieve to a point, sure. But you won't thrive and be the greatest version of yourself while you're so afraid to let your foot off the gas.

The problem with perfectionism is that it's unattainable and unsustainable, rendering it a hindrance to success. "Perfectionism is a narrow, intolerant expectation that we will never make mistakes or have any imperfections," writes Sharon Martin, MSW, LCSW, author of *The CBT Workbook for Perfectionism*. "We take one mistake and use it to deem ourselves complete failures or inferior...When we expect perfection, we'll inevitably be disappointed. We all make mistakes, no matter how smart we are or how hard we work."[1] It's stressful to have so much at stake, to think that we have to deliver perfection in order to be seen as an indispensable part of a team, a worthy new hire, or deserving of that promotion. Unmeetable standards set us up for failure because even if we come close, flawlessness is not achievable. And the more discrepant our reality is from our expectations, the more distress we'll feel. So, unachievable expectations can cause such chronic anxiety and self-doubt that they stymie our progress and ascent.

In her book *The Gifts of Imperfection*, thought leader Brené Brown, PhD, MSW, references how research shows that perfectionism actually *hampers* success and can lead to anxiety, depression, and what she calls "life-paralysis." That's the fallout from "all of the opportunities we miss because we're too afraid to put anything out in the world that could be imperfect...all of the dreams that we don't follow because of our deep fear of failing, making mistakes, and disappointing others."[2] It's crucial to remember that, because we are human, we *will* make mistakes. That's a fact. That's why we have to recalibrate our expectations to acknowledge reality if we want to keep moving forward to achieve our goals.

This doesn't mean that we must settle either for mediocrity or for an insular life of perpetual worry. *Fun times!* There's another way to keep ourselves from getting mired in pursuit of this albatross, to escape the self-sabotaging cycle of anxiety and standards by which we are doomed to fail. The antidote comes in the form of a different metric for success: *excellence*. The bar is still extraordinarily high—where we like it!—but this time it allows for our humanity.

THE EXCELLENCE EQUATION

Excellence hinges on honoring yourself, mind, body, and spirit, holding space for a range of what success looks like rather than some perfect-or-bust mindset.

Each person is unique and will manifest excellence in their own way, within a day, a year, or a lifetime. So that we have a shared understanding, the working definition we'll use is what I call the "Excellence Equation," which outlines the overall concept in simple terms:

EXCELLENCE = HAPPY, HEALTHY, AND HIGH-ACHIEVING

> **Happy:** Stable mood, a sense of peace and freedom, hope, experiencing and moving through a full range of feelings, no emotion being denied, judged, or perpetually stuck in. Definitely not continual anxiety, worry, panic, or depression. Actively optimizing your thoughts and behaviors to reduce distress and promote well-being.
>
> **Healthy:** Getting ample sleep and regular physical activity, eating well, effectively managing stress, not using substances to numb out, taking care of yourself by attending appropriate medical visits.
>
> **High-Achieving:** Sustainably striving for meaningful goals, cultivating and maintaining strong relationships, being

a part of something bigger than yourself, and continuing to learn and grow (not settling for stagnation) while also appreciating what you already have. Moving forward, making progress, and persevering in the pursuit of purposeful accomplishments.

After all, would it really be an excellent life if you were walking around feeling chronically anxious and unfulfilled, disregarding your mental and physical well-being, not using your energy to accomplish anything meaningful, living in isolation, and thinking you didn't have anything to be grateful for?

Creating an excellent life means making your mind (Happy), body (Healthy), and spirit (High-Achieving) of paramount importance.

WHY WE SEEK PERFECTION

Most of us understand at least intellectually that no human is perfect, and perfection, therefore, is not a real metric. Not only that, but the very concept of perfection depends on who is defining it. Our understanding of the term may be so ingrained that we assume it's an objective standard that everyone would agree upon; that it's above reproach. But the truth is: Different people define "perfect" differently. And we can't control the judgments and beliefs of others, only ourselves. So even if we do a "perfect" job, what's to stop someone else from coming in and finding flaws, reasons why something isn't good enough? Why *we* aren't good enough?

We need to ask ourselves where our standards come from.

Perfectionism, however we may individually define "perfection," is fundamentally about gaining approval—something we high achievers often chase. It feeds on our fears of failure and rejection, of not measuring up, and breeds feelings of inadequacy and even shame. As a result, it often prevents us from taking necessary risks, advancing, learning, and excelling. As I often say, "Perfectionism is the Achilles' heel of the ambitious." So why do we, as high achievers, pursue perfection, even when we know it's like chasing the horizon?

Over the years, I have noticed three primary issues that hook my patients on the illusion of perfection: the Comparison Trap, Failure Seems Fatal, and the Desire to Be Valued. Let's take them one at a time.

The Comparison Trap

It's Saturday morning and you're scrolling through Instagram when you come upon a post from a peer in your field. The photograph features this person (read: perceived competitor) smiling big and looking immaculate while receiving an award from some celebrity or bigwig in the industry. The accompanying caption is a humble brag like, "Wow. My mind is blown. So honored to be recognized by such spectacular folks last night. What a magical night! I could never have done it without my team. #noiinteam"

After you're done dry heaving, you're immediately thrust into a cyclone of anxiety and feelings of failure. This person clearly has a perfect life! She's fit, good-looking, well dressed, and obviously killing it at work. You wonder: "Why haven't I had that kind of success? Why isn't my wardrobe as cool? I clearly haven't worked hard enough! Why am I so flawed?"

This is a pitfall for many high achievers. Even Oprah—the ultimate success story—has talked about measuring herself against Barbara Walters in her early career to her own detriment. "This will save you. Stop comparing yourself to other people," she said during a University of Southern California commencement speech in 2018. "You're only on this planet to be you."[3]

Sometimes that's easier said than done. High achievers chronically believe that other people are perfect, so they need to be perfect, too. In my office, I find myself reminding patients again and again that the picture people project isn't necessarily aligned with reality. After all, if you're posting images with filters on *your* social media feeds, curating the most flattering photos that suggest the greatest level of accomplishment, how much of a leap is it to theorize that the people you're putting on a pedestal are doing the same? People post pictures of their best selves. What don't they post? Photos of the times they've come home after a long day to discover they forgot to go grocery shopping and have nothing but ketchup in the fridge. Or when their photogenic baby wakes up screaming for the third night in a row or pukes all over those adorable sheets in the new nursery they were just showing off. Or when all those seemingly enviable business trips lead to struggles with insomnia and dysregulated eating and exercise schedules. Or when they fight with their partner. People's lives might appear effortless, like they're always winning. That's what we're so often conditioned to believe others value and want to see online, so that's what people deliver. But the true experience of their everyday is a mystery.

Standards that are based on smoke and mirrors—these airbrushed pseudo-realities—are unmeetable because they're fabricated, and they can prompt inaccurate, unbalanced perceptions of others—and of yourself. This distorted thinking, often associated with the All-or-Nothing Thinking in the Troublesome Trifecta we discussed in Part One, has you shining your flashlight on all the ways someone else appears perfect and on all your flaws: "I must be perfect or I won't be lovable. If I can't be perfect like they are, I am a failure."

I often say, "Put anyone on my couch." Everyone has issues to talk about: difficult family relationships, challenging marriages, things they wish they could change about themselves, traumatic pasts, or uncertain futures. Interestingly, the people who appear to have the most perfect lives often actually have the most to unpack. Within the safety of my four walls, they confess to being besieged with self-doubt and imposter syndrome. And the minute they have a success, like that honor they've just plastered all over social media, they're panicking about what's next, questioning if they can live up to the hype. They wonder, "Am I even ready for this next step?" The responsibilities of this new promotion, the demands of a job after graduation? They're insecure—just like you.

When you start playing the "How shiny is *your* apple?" game, every currency is fodder for self-scrutiny and comparison. Your salary, number of publications, relationship status, amount of grant funding, wrinkles, waist size, marathon speed, type of car—it's all suddenly imperfect. You feel not good enough in contrast with whomever you've deemed the ideal. And no one ever wins this game. There is always more money to be had, a higher title to hold, more distinguished honors and medals to win, and bigger houses to own.

These social comparisons further reinforce that unhealthy desire to continue striving for perfection, the idea that good is not good enough. "I'm so far behind, what if I never catch up?"

TAKE ACTION

Consider how the Comparison Trap shows up in your own life.

Think of an example in which someone outshined you and left you feeling less-than. In the vein of that award recipient on Instagram, perhaps a coworker got promoted, a colleague got published in an important journal, or a sibling landed a higher salary than you or got engaged first. Notice: What did you tell yourself? How did that make you feel? How did it impact your behaviors?

For example:

Thoughts: "Look at how perfect [smart/successful/better] they are. I need to be more like them. I'm not as good as I thought I was. I'm such a disappointment."

Feelings: Insecure, anxious, stressed, unworthy, frantic, defeated.

Behaviors: Perfection-seeking behaviors to try to compensate. At the office, you may start logging more hours when you're already feeling overloaded to try to prove your worth. You train harder and post pictures that make you seem like you're thriving, hustling to "measure up" or accumulate more likes—all the while shining your flashlight of attention on what others are doing instead of doing your personal best.

Now you try!

Thoughts:

Feelings:

Behaviors:

ASK DR. A

Question: Is social comparison always detrimental?

Dr. A: Nope, that would be All-or-Nothing Thinking. Comparing yourself with others can be beneficial if it inspires, encourages, or empowers you. If seeing what they've been able to accomplish helps you feel that you could achieve great things, too—that's awesome. But if you're focusing on all the things others have done that you haven't, leaving yourself overwhelmed, envious, frustrated, or

> unconfident, that's your inner GPS—your feelings—notifying you that you've fallen into the Comparison Trap. And it's time to reroute!

Failure Seems Fatal

Failure Seems Fatal is the second perfectionist hook. This All-or-Nothing Thinking hijacks you into believing that, if you fail, you'll never accomplish your dreams and all of your hard work will be wasted. Rather than perceiving a setback as a momentary blip, a challenge that can be navigated, or even (yes!) an opportunity to learn, this polarized thinking makes any mistake seem like total life-ending defeat.

As a high achiever, you set big, ambitious goals and you want to do everything you can to achieve them. That's great! But as a result, you may have convinced yourself that you can't afford to let down your guard for even a moment—that any misstep or mistake, any laxness, may lead to unbearable consequences. Therefore, perfection is literally the only option.

I had one patient, Charles, who notably struggled with this issue. An attorney working on an important case, he admitted to being paralyzed by overwhelm and dread. "Dr. A," he said, "if I don't win this case, it won't just be disappointing. My career will be over!" Charles viewed any mistake as failure and any failure as apocalyptic. Can you relate?

It's important to acknowledge the reality that sometimes there *are* negative consequences for not winning a case, or getting a B on a test, or striking out in the big game—but they're not usually as dire or high-stakes as high achievers anticipate. The truth is that things typically play out much worse in our heads than they do in our lives. There are more solutions than we might at first realize during tough moments. And I'm here to teach you ways to cope during those challenging times.

The Desire to Be Valued

We all want to feel loved and know that we matter—it's fundamental to our humanity. And it's also the most insidious reason high achievers are intent on reaching perfection. They've been led to believe they must *earn* that love or prove their worth, that their value is tied to what they can accomplish, not who they are. Where does this come from? In addition to the societal messages with which we are all bombarded, you may have parents, coaches, teachers, bosses, and other influential people in your life who have communicated, either directly or inadvertently, that you "should" strive for perfection—and that you should want to. Anything less is simply unacceptable. Sometimes being the best is how high achievers got positive attention from their parents, especially if their parents were emotionally distant, narcissistic, overwhelmed, or high-achieving, too. Perhaps you began equating parental praise, approval, and affection with unmitigated achievement or winning. Or you heard your caregivers and people you looked up to criticize or devalue people who weren't doing things exactly "right." It taught you a quintessential all-or-nothing message: Only perfect people are lovable.

Many of my patients begin our initial session by admitting they know deep down that they are somehow "defective," "damaged," or "a disappointment." No matter how many times I hear people say that, it still tugs at my heart. They describe the harsh judgments they grew up with: *What's wrong with you?* or *Why can't you be more like so-and-so's son or daughter?* The critical reactions, exasperated sighs, shame, rejection, or even punishment they received for being less than the best. Messages that they are not okay as they are. Thus, perfectionism became their compensatory strategy for winning the love, approval, and acceptance of others. The issue is that these are basic human needs that can't be turned off. That's why perfection feels so make-or-break for folks who learned that flawlessness was their only route to get those basic needs met. And now they're not maximizing their potential because they don't feel good about themselves.

So how can we learn to feel better about ourselves and detach self-worth from achievement? I have seen entire lives transformed by the eventual acceptance of certain fundamental truths:

First and foremost, if you make your internal worth beholden to external validation, you will live with chronic anxiety.

Read it again.

While your accomplishments are important in their own right, you are *not* your achievements. You are not your awards, education, bank account, looks, or possessions. It may feel hokey, but you deserve happiness simply because you're human. Many of my clients have trouble believing this and so I posit this extreme example: If I told you five ants were just killed outside your door, you might feel bad, but you'd move on with your day. Conversely, if I said five people were just killed outside your door, would those scenarios feel different? We understand on a visceral level that people matter—we are more than just ants! Even if we have trouble applying that concept to ourselves.

TAKE ACTION

Repeat after me: *I matter. I have value. I am a living, breathing human being whose happiness matters.* You matter. As. You. Are. Now. And you always will. No one can take that away from you. Not your boss, your family, your romantic partner, your teachers or coaches, your audience, your coworkers, your critics, your friends, or your foes. Not even yourself.

I want to be clear: I am not asking you to sacrifice your drive, talent, ambition, passion, or commitment. If you're reading this book, you are goal-oriented and hardworking and you really, really care about what you are doing with your life. So believing you are inherently valuable and ending your quest for perfection is not going to suddenly make you apathetic, mediocre, or stagnant. That's just not who you are. Your drive isn't going anywhere. What you are going to become is less anxious and less stymied by fear and worry. It's the difference between living under the weight of perfectionism's suffocating pressure, unrelenting demands, and constant feelings of inadequacy, as opposed to feeling the freedom to be who you are and take good care of yourself while working toward meaningful goals as you strive for excellence.

A POWERFUL PARADOX

Often my clients express worry that, if they release the perfection metric and its accompanying anxiety, they might become lazy, lose their edge, and not reach their goals. They feel as though the unattainable standards and discomfort are motivating them to perform exceptionally.

This is a pervasive and dangerous misconception. The truth is that shifting from trying to be perfect to working for excellence actually *protects* and *enhances* your edge. Why? Because insistence on perfection leads to burnout, which diminishes you. We both know that when you're exhausted, overworked, and overwhelmed, you're not at your most productive, focused, or high-achieving. And you don't feel good about yourself.

Battles are won and lost in your mind. Imagine you're talking to a friend who is struggling. You wouldn't berate them for their imperfections! You would try to energize them by being encouraging and underlining their strengths, because that's what might help. This is the way you need to talk to yourself if you want to be successful, too.

Knowing that you matter and that mistakes don't render you less valuable makes you the *opposite* of lazy. It activates you. You'll seize opportunities. Be more innovative and industrious. And you will work harder—now in a more balanced way—not because you're trying to prove yourself but because you're not hampered by anxiety and setting yourself up to fail with an unmeetable metric of success. You're free to try new things, to experiment, to work hard outside such narrow confines. You can be excellent and still take chances, discover passions and new skills. Case in point, I have countless clients who chose their college major and career path based on what their parents wanted in hopes of garnering approval. And they hate it! The minute we manage to free them up to pursue excellence based on their own standards, I have seen them explore all kinds of things that enliven them and empower them to achieve fantastic professional success—from astrophysics to zoology!

This is the powerful paradox: Once you separate your self-worth from your achievements and give yourself permission to be human (which you will be anyway), you'll be able to accomplish more than you ever thought possible—because you won't be so afraid anymore. You may be shaking your head in doubt, you high achiever! It's true! That chronic anxiety and fear of failure has been eating away at your energy, blocking your path to growth and greatness.

THE EXCELLENCE SOLUTION

Remember that handy equation earlier in the chapter? Excellence is the pursuit of achievement, while also honoring our mental (happy) and physical (healthy) well-being. It's seeking success without it impacting our belief in our self-worth. The fundamental difference between striving for excellence and striving for perfection is that excellence allows us the grace to make mistakes. And we need that because, as we've learned, when you're trying so hard to be perfect—to be seen as the smartest, strongest, most accomplished, or even coolest—you wind up saddled with immense anxiety and insecurity, making you less productive. These expectations can render you afraid of trying new things, taking risks, speaking up in meetings, or reaching out to others for help—because you fear appearing incompetent, foolish, weak, or worse, "stupid." You may even underperform during key moments or procrastinate due to the tremendous pressure you've put on yourself.

Or inadvertently, you may be pigeonholed as a person who doesn't switch gears easily, gets bogged down with trivial details, and doesn't respond well to feedback—no doubt the very opposite of how you want to appear to others.

Excellence is the key to escaping chronic fear of failure while continuing to be a high achiever who shines. It's not an invitation to lower your standards. It's the opposite. The goal is to hold high expectations without denigrating yourself for every error.

But switching from pursuing perfection to pursuing the more advantageous excellence requires a shift in your thinking. Perfection is rigid, while excellence is flexible. With perfection, the problem isn't that we want to push ourselves or continually be our best selves, it's that we think we must only be the best and our best can never vary. Excellence allows us to embrace the fact that our "best" will differ by the day. Think coping with jet lag, a cold, heartbreak. Ultimately, your best can be outstanding, but you can't *always* be at 100 percent. To believe you'll *never* make an error, lose, or fail will just lead you to feel stressed, frustrated, impatient, exhausted, and deflated. Aspiring for excellence, where you do your very best while also understanding that your non-deity status means you are fallible, empowers you to move forward with more motivation and less anxiety. And it allows for more than one "right" way to do things, clearing the path for innovation, growth, learning, creativity, and expansion. Excellence prioritizes progress over people-pleasing. This means valuing gains like additional knowledge, expertise, and skills—the process—instead of focusing solely on the outcome.

Counter to the rigidity of perfectionism, excellence offers a more useful, balanced stance: Instead of fearing mistakes, we can acknowledge the reality that they will occur and *use* them to our advantage as opportunities to gain insight, problem-solve, pivot, and generate improved strategies for success. Use the chart below to assess whether you've been working toward excellence or perfection:

Perfection	Excellence
I have unrealistic standards and expectations for myself and others.	I have high standards and expectations for myself and others.
I constantly feel like I'm running behind and on fumes.	I feel continually energized by my progress.
I feel limited by the rigid definition of success imposed upon me by myself and others.	I have limitless possibilities for growth.
I think mistakes are absolutely unacceptable.	I don't like making mistakes, but I know they're opportunities to learn.
I think failing at a goal means *I* am a failure.	I think failing at a goal only means I failed at that specific goal.
I am focused solely on the outcome.	I value both process *and* outcome.
I'm living at a harried, unsustainable pace.	I'm working hard at a sustainable pace.
I have a fixed idea of what's "best."	I have a fluid concept of "best" that evolves based on circumstances.
The pressure on me stifles my motivation and creativity.	The freedom I feel boosts my motivation and encourages curiosity and creativity.
I'm on a fast track to burnout.	I am filled with energy for the many facets of my life.

Perfection	Excellence
My mindset breeds competition and resentment.	My mindset fosters collaboration and appreciation.
My primary desire is to please people.	My primary desire is to make progress.
I often feel disappointed in my life.	I often feel satisfied by my life.

POKING HOLES IN PRESSURE-COOKER THINKING

Okay, Dr. A, so how do I shift my mind from wanting to be perfect to striving for excellence? Great news! You're already developing these skills. The transformation from perfectionism to pursuing excellence happens when we learn to identify and poke holes in All-or-Nothing Thinking, or what I call Pressure-Cooker Thinking.

You got this.

When you notice that your flashlight is shining on all-or-nothing thoughts (always/never, everything/nothing, perfect/terrible), you know to take aim, ask questions to poke holes in those suckers, and then use new and improved self-talk. This is the path to excellence!

Let's walk through the steps specifically with regard to perfectionism.

First, you notice where you're shining your flashlight.

If you're having many thoughts, try to identify the chief offender: Which thought is making you the *most* anxious? For example, one patient of mine, Sarah, who was enormously successful in her career, was really struggling with being single. Despite her achievements, she diminished herself because of her romantic status. She felt she was failing unless she was part of a "perfect couple." "All my friends are in serious relationships," she would say, shoulders tensed. "Some of them are already getting married—and I don't have anyone! I'm a total loser." She felt like everyone else was able to find their perfect match. Why was she all alone? When Sarah and I talked through her anxiety, she identified the thought that was making her feel the worst: "I'm a total loser." That All-or-Nothing Thinking decreased her confidence and hindered her progress, as she began feeling anxious while using dating apps and avoiding attending college alumni events because she didn't want to say she was single. As long as she was negating the fullness of who she was by fixating on what she thought she lacked, there was no way she was going to show up as her best self.

Next, we worked to poke holes in that perfectionist All-or-Nothing Thinking, asking, "How is this thought *not necessarily* true?" Yes, Sarah was single. That was a fact. But she was forcing a dichotomy: Either she was partnered up or she was worthless.

When you notice you're in an all-or-nothing trap, these specific questions can help you poke holes:

- **Is there a more balanced option that I could consider?**
- **Are there examples of when something different occurred that disprove my polarized thinking?**
- **Am I holding myself to unrealistic standards?**

As Sarah reflected on these questions, she recognized that, yes, there was a more balanced option. That she simply hadn't met the right person yet and her life didn't need to be tied up in a "perfect" bow by a certain age. That her friends' committed relationships might appear perfect, but she knew better from many a heart-to-heart. And no, she wasn't a "total loser," because she had built a life full of a lot of other amazing things, including a thriving career, a robust friend group, and a home she adored. She realized she knew people who weren't in committed relationships whom she admired. And finally, yes, she was holding herself to unrealistic standards because finding a romantic partner is something that can take time and she didn't need to rely on the social armament of being a "we" to be enough.

Relief dawning on her face, she said, "I've made my relationship status the defining feature of my life and told myself it would *always* be this way. I realize now that isn't the case."

Finally, it was time for Sarah to craft a balanced, believable thought to replace her cognitive distortion that could act as a reset when self-doubt and perfectionism popped up again. She needed a Twist of Hope or, as we discussed, an honest look at the reality of the unhelpful thought with a realistic positive spin at the end.

So instead of "I'm a total loser," Sarah and I brainstormed and generated this improved inner monologue, honoring her concerns: "I really want to be in a happy, committed relationship, *but* I know people who are single and have great lives, and I have many good things in my life. No one thing could ever make me a 'total loser.' I may not *always* be single anyway, but no matter what, my value isn't defined by my relationship status." Focusing on what was easiest to remember and what resonated the most, we developed this short sticky-note-friendly statement: "My relationship status doesn't define me."

Now it's *your* turn to poke holes in and overcome one of your all-or-nothing perfectionist thoughts. Use the three-step process you just learned to successfully conquer your pressure-cooker thought in the Take Action here.

TAKE ACTION

Identify one all-or-nothing thought you had recently. Think about the situation in which you had the thought, how the thought made you feel, and in what ways it kept you stuck.

Next, ask yourself these questions to collect your evidence:

- How is my thought *not necessarily* true?
- Is there a more balanced option to consider?
- Am I beating myself up for making a human mistake?
- Am I tying my self-worth to my performance, appearance, or achievement?
- Am I holding myself to unrealistic standards?
- Is this thought about unattainable perfection or about excellence?
- Are there any exceptions, when something different did occur, that disprove my always/never thought?
- Did I lose perspective?
- What might a trusted friend or mentor say about my thought?

Create your new and improved thought and practice saying it out loud at least three times today. Then, mentally or out loud, say it anytime your all-or-nothing thought pops into your mind. Notice how you feel after saying the new thought. If it's a believable, balanced thought, you will begin to feel better. If not, keep working to craft one that feels both accurate and helpful.

YOUR BEHAVIORS MATTER

An excellent life is created by continually optimizing both our thoughts *and* our behaviors. Remember, feelings, thoughts, and behaviors are inexorably linked, so in order to feel our best and do our best, we need to make sure our thoughts and behaviors are supporting us. For instance, if Sarah wants to meet someone and now she's shifted her thinking to a more productive and excellent standard, she can take steps toward making that a reality. She can join or revisit a dating app, tell friends she's looking to meet someone, or even talk to that cute person she keeps seeing at the coffee shop.

The opposite is also true. If Sarah hadn't shifted her thoughts and was still telling herself she was a "total loser," there's very little chance that she'd have the confidence or energy to put herself out there. After all, if she doesn't see value in herself, how can she believe others might value her, too?

It's not enough to rework our self-talk to avoid perfectionist pitfalls. We also have to consider our behaviors. And for perfectionist high achievers, the most common, unhelpful, anxiety-promoting behavior is *avoidance*.

Avoidance is choosing not to confront the cause of your anxiety—which only makes your anxiety worse. It prevents you from learning how to face and manage your fears, and it also instigates unhelpful thoughts. For example, maybe you dream of becoming a published author but then think, "What if my writing isn't good? People will think less of me," which makes you feel anxious, so you stop writing or avoid ever sharing your work with anyone. Maybe you crumple it up and throw every attempt in the trash, like we discussed earlier. Your avoidant behavior then cycles back into negatively impacting your thoughts: "I'm not really a writer. I've never even published anything. I'll never publish anything." These thoughts keep amplifying your anxiety and decrease the likelihood of taking the necessary action to move toward your goal. Avoidance—which often manifests as procrastination—will keep you stuck.

ASK DR. A

Question: If I really care about doing my best, why do I procrastinate so much?

Dr. A: Honestly, I hear this one a lot from my patients. High achievers like you want so badly to do things "right" or perfectly that you psych yourself out. Your assignment or project becomes a mental behemoth—so huge, so consequential that you don't know where to start. So you don't, as a result of a paralyzing combination of perfectionism, self-doubt about your ability, and ramped-up anxiety. As I like to say, "Perfection is the enemy of done!" Next time you find yourself procrastinating, try this:

- Turn off that pressure cooker! Remind yourself that you're striving for *excellence*, not perfection. Your project can be excellent without being flawless.
- Strategically "chunk" your big project into bite-size pieces that feel more approachable.
- Do one thing right away: Create a document or brainstorm some bullet points. The quicker you can overcome inertia even with something small, the faster you'll increase your confidence, triumph over procrastination, and complete your work—with ample time *before* the deadline.

Approach is the most efficient antidote to avoidance. But as simple as it sounds, for high achievers, it often feels difficult. Reasonably, it may seem counterintuitive to lean into a situation that is making you feel anxious. Unfortunately, sidestepping the elephant in the room can exacerbate your anxiety, as it sits in the back of your mind, looming larger and larger: "Maybe I'll never write again!" If you keep avoiding what you're afraid of, you'll keep feeling afraid.

In other words: Avoidance perpetuates anxiety. Approach overcomes anxiety.

Throughout my years as a psychologist, one thing I've observed is that people tend to *vastly* overestimate how much discomfort they will feel if they face their fears—especially versus the anxiety they're already causing themselves with avoidance. As Albert Einstein said, "The only source of knowledge is experience." You won't know you can face your fears and tolerate discomfort until you try. The anticipation is the hardest part! In order to get unstuck, feel less anxious, and move forward, you must be willing to take action. And for you, that might mean accepting potential imperfection.

As basketball legend Michael Jordan once said, "Don't be afraid to fail. Be afraid not to try." In order for you to enjoy the impact of excellence versus perfection, you do need to begin to accept mistakes. But Rome wasn't built in a day. Just try something! Instead of crumpling up your work and stomping away, look at it again and ask yourself: What about this *did* work? Consider trying again and, in that way, subtly shifting your mindset. You don't have to take action that stretches you so far outside your comfort zone that it overwhelms you. Again, this isn't an all-or-nothing approach. Take baby steps. What is the next step that feels *doable*? Send an email to a colleague at the same level without belaboring it. Sit with being okay with a typo. If you're a writer who is stuck or fearful of submitting work, perhaps sign up for a class or hire a writing coach. You can slowly begin to make changes.

Taking action doesn't necessarily mean everything will turn out exactly as you want, but it will end your anxiety paralysis. It's better to have something come out differently than you wanted than not to materialize at all. There are real negative consequences to not submitting or trying something because of a fear that it's not perfect. And there are real potential benefits to putting yourself and your work out there. If you don't try, you'll never know, which equals regret and missed opportunities. By approaching instead of avoiding what you fear, you'll be better able to handle what comes next. You're driven, determined, and hardworking as a high achiever. You inherently possess the capacity to do this. And once you do, there's no limit to your excellence.

TAKE ACTION

To truly conquer a perfection-or-bust mindset, you need to know from experience you can make mistakes while learning something new. So for this Take Action, I encourage you to pick one thing that you've put off or been afraid to do because you might not look smart, cool, or proficient.

This can be any activity you want! Take a pottery, dance, coding, or improv class, perform at an open mic, or belt out some karaoke! ("Eye of the Tiger," anyone?) Attend a conference or retreat that previously seemed out of reach or join an online foreign-language club. Go sailing, fly-fishing, golfing, or surfing. Learn how to play pickleball or an instrument.

I personally love traveling to new places, attempting to navigate unfamiliar roads, and asking locals for their suggestions of where to go for food and fun. There's no way to look sophisticated, erudite, or perfect while doing that, no matter how hard you try. Whatever you choose, remember that the goal is to show yourself that you can tolerate (and maybe even enjoy!) doing something new that you're not instantly adept at.

Pro Tip: If you find yourself struggling in the moment, try focusing your attention on the activity you are doing and not on yourself. Rather than shining your flashlight on judging your skill level, how you may appear, or how you compare with others, focus on your actions. Accept that to learn something new means being a beginner (not your comfortable expert role). This is the road to an excellent life!

For Essential #1, the goal is to release perfectionism and strive for excellence in order to dispel limiting anxiety and get at the root of what's holding you back. That means embracing your own value instead of comparing yourself to others, poking holes in unhelpful all-or-nothing self-talk, and allowing yourself to approach the unknown. You're already doing an *excellent* job!

TOP TAKEAWAYS

- Perfectionism is the Achilles' heel of the ambitious.
- Beware the Comparison Trap.
- If you make your internal worth beholden to external validation, you will live with chronic anxiety.
- Remember: You are not an ant! You have inherent human worth—and it's not tied to your accomplishments, appearance, or performance.
- Excellence allows space for high achievement *and* your humanity!
- Approach is the most efficient antidote to avoidance. Don't be afraid to be a beginner!

ESSENTIAL #2

INVEST IN THE ULTIMATE CURRENCY: YOUR ENERGY

The greatest wealth is health.

—Virgil

So you've begun your *excellent* adventure, leaving perfectionism in the dust. That's a crucial step on the road to establishing enduring high achievement.

Now you need to ensure that you have the energy to sustain your excellence. You do that by prioritizing self-care.

I know, I know. Right now you might be rolling your eyes and muttering, "Seriously, Dr. A? Self-care?"

Yep. Not only am I serious, but self-care is serious business. Far from being extraneous fluff, it's what will fuel you with the strength and stamina you need to be high-performing in the short term and be your most excellent self in the long term. That's right: Self-care is how you address and optimize the Healthy element of your Excellence Equation.

I get the reticence. I really do. In recent years, self-care has become synonymous with self-indulgence in the vein of bubble baths and chakra alignment. But that's not necessarily the kind of self-care I mean (though I'm all for whatever helps *you*). I'm simply talking about taking care of yourself on a regular basis, so you can show up as your most energetic, focused, and motivated self. Even if you're someone who prides yourself on needing no sleep and living on enormous amounts of coffee, you still have finite energy and you're going to hit the wall. So you need to recharge your batteries and replenish your energy reserves with quality sleep, exercise, moments of relaxation, enjoyable activities, healthy foods, and plenty of hydration. That's how you're going to function at your best.

BURNOUT IS REAL

You're exhausted and unfocused. Every task feels like an uphill battle. Instead of enthusiastic, you feel depleted and impatient.

Sound familiar? Probably.

Sound fun? Not at all.

Since most anxious high achievers tell themselves they must always be productive, must always prove themselves, and must be "perfect" (yep, there's that pesky perfectionism again!), they're particularly prone to burnout. The buildup of chronic stress leaves them feeling drained, diminished, and overwhelmed. My patients are a chorus of:

> *"I feel so worn out all the time."*
> *"I dread going to work at this point."*
> *"I'm just irritated by my work."*
> *"I don't feel as productive as usual."*
> *"I'm not even sure I'm doing a good job."*

The bottom line is they've run out of juice. And like their overtaxed electronics, without an influx of energy, they'll power down.

Beating burnout is possible, but I do want to be clear: It's not always possible to prevent or heal burnout through self-care practices and routines alone. Sometimes workplace burnout may occur because of a "mismatch between a person and the circumstances of a job,"[1] according to Christina Maslach, PhD, professor of psychology (emerita) at the University of California, Berkeley. If you're dealing with unrealistic managerial expectations, poor communication between colleagues, a lack of control over your own work, or insufficient staffing or resources, self-care might mean making strategic changes at work or even looking for a new job that's a better fit. Either way, burnout is not something you need to face alone. If the stress is too great, a trained mental health professional can offer much-needed support.

"YES, BUT..."

When I explain the benefits of self-care to my high-achieving clients, they do become more open to it. But even knowing that self-care enhances their edge, or that it has a positive ripple effect, or that it's a powerful defense against burnout, I still hear a lot of "yes, but..." replies from my clients. The reasons they resist can seem like compelling, rational excuses: "I literally can't go on vacation; I have deadlines to meet!" Or, "There's no way I can get to bed on time; I have a proposal to finish tonight!"

Odds are you're making "yes, but..." rationalizations without even realizing! By now we've learned that if something is a thought, we can identify it, examine it, and—most important—remember that it may not necessarily be true. Before we get into some real talk about how to add self-care behaviors to your routine, we need to poke some holes in those "yes, but..." thoughts. Grab your flashlight! And let's take a look at the four most common categories of self-care excuses.

I Don't Have the Time

I hear this refrain constantly and I get it. When you're stressed out about performing or accomplishing myriad tasks, the last thing you want to do is take a break! What if you lose momentum? Or your boss sees? Or you really feel that you can't add even one more thing to your plate right now, no matter how important people say it is for your health? In truth, making time to do something as brief and basic as taking a walk can actually *sharpen* your edge. According to a 2014 Stanford University study,[2] walking can increase creative output "by an average of 60 percent," and "creative juices continued to flow even when a person sat back down shortly after a walk."[3] And this doesn't mean you have to squeeze in hour-long hikes between meetings. A fifteen-minute stroll around the block—or even on a treadmill—can yield notable results.[4] So, keep it moving to keep innovating!

TAKE ACTION

Don't let your jam-packed schedule become a roadblock! I know that when you're overextended, trying to schedule routine doctor's appointments, workouts, or even grocery shopping can be a logistical challenge.

For example, my patient Liz, who you'll remember prioritized getting her hair highlighted over her dental hygiene, sheepishly confessed that it had been almost two years since she'd been to the dentist. When she finally went, she had two new cavities—which required even more of her time. Like Liz, busy high achievers often wait to book self-care until a health concern balloons. But you can prevent unnecessary suffering by being proactive.

If you haven't already, schedule your doctor and dental appointments in advance, strategically building in time with purposeful intention.

Now is the time to ask yourself: Have you had your annual physical this year? Have you visited the dentist in the last six to twelve months? If not, call and make an appointment.

Isn't Self-Care Selfish?

Not. At. All. Self-care is necessary for all humans, especially those seeking long-lasting excellence. After all, you can't win the Grand Prix without fuel!

There's an important distinction to be made between selfishness and self-care. Selfish acts benefit you to the detriment of others. Conversely, self-care benefits you *and* others. We're all acquainted with the metaphor about putting on our own oxygen masks first, so we are better equipped to help others. But I have always felt that there's a missed consideration there. Most important, we need to put on our own oxygen masks first because we *deserve* to breathe! This is an especially essential concept for high achievers, who are even less likely to feel deserving of that breath unless they believe they've earned it and who don't want to admit they need an oxygen mask in the first place.

Similarly, you need to put your own self-care first because you *deserve* to honor your health—*and* to have energy for your relationships with everyone from loved ones to colleagues to neighbors. Taking care of yourself initiates the positive ripple effect of self-care.

I Need to "Earn" My Self-Care

This is a big one. Many harried patients tell me they haven't yet achieved enough to deserve a break, hedging, "Maybe I'll start prioritizing myself after I complete this one last assignment." And you can imagine what happens from there—another project and then another. As an anxious high achiever, you may believe you've got to suffer to be successful, that you must sacrifice your well-being to prove you're indispensable. This is an unhealthy, self-reinforcing cycle that perpetuates your propensity to put off self-care.

And there's a problem with only implementing self-care *after* you've achieved your goals. For one thing, the goalpost is always moving. As a high achiever, you'll always find another hill to climb. But also your *ability* to be successful is what suffers when you don't take care of yourself. And you can't sustain success on a single charge, no matter how high-performance your battery. In reality, pausing to refuel—with a brain-boosting snack, a glass of water, a walk, or a quick chat with a friend—replenishes your energy and helps you finish a project strong. I personally don't approach a workday without a protein drink, a big mug of green tea, and copious dark chocolate handy.

Most important, you're not an ant, remember? You don't have to *earn* your self-care. You deserve to take good care of yourself because you are human. Your health and happiness matter. You matter.

Lastly, because behaviors impact thoughts, showing yourself that you matter by taking care of yourself can improve how you think about yourself. Doing self-care is concrete evidence that you *can* make time for yourself. The behavior of going to the doctor's appointment or to the supermarket for healthy food or buying tickets to see your favorite band so you have something nice to look forward to demonstrates that you are worthy of spending time, money, and energy to feel good. These behaviors, how you actively honor your inherent worth, inform how you think about yourself.

All together now! Better self-care = better self-talk.

I Don't Need It, I'll Be Fine

High achievers often minimize their exhaustion and overwhelm, claiming it's unavoidable or pointing to someone else who is "easily" maintaining under the same pressures. "I'll be fine, Dr. A," they say, "as soon as this project is over." It's hard sometimes to recognize the warning signs of burnout until they negatively impact your mood, energy, and ability to continue functioning at the highest level. Stay aware!

Consistently incorporating self-care that feels doable and enjoyable will help ward off burnout.

Okay! Now that you've conquered these "yes, but..." thoughts, it's time to strategically invest in the self-care fundamentals with the greatest payoff for your success and well-being.

PUTTING THE S.E.L.F. IN SELF-CARE

So where to start with self-care? Well, to put it simply, you're going to start with your S.E.L.F.: Sleep, Exercise, Look Forward, and Fuel. Each one of these fundamentals helps you maximize and sustain your energy so you can be healthy, happy, and high-achieving. No doubt you've heard a variation on these themes before, but I know a lot of my clients still struggle to fit them into their lives. Rather than focusing on ever more creative and challenging self-care strategies, I want you to focus on making sure your daily habits are healthy, doable, and consistent. Let's have at it!

Sleep

For high achievers, getting a good night's sleep is absolutely critical. Research shows that chronic lack of sleep has negative effects on memory, attention, concentration, and our ability to make decisions. Insufficient rest has been linked to poor work performance, increased risk of health issues (such as high blood pressure, diabetes, and obesity), and problems with mood and relationships.[5] On the other hand, getting good sleep—at least seven hours a night for adults[6]—can improve your productivity, problem-solving skills, memory, and concentration.[7]

As much as you may wish differently, good sleep is essential.

I recall one patient, Danielle, who—after upping her sleep from four or five hours to a consistent seven a night—was not only more effective at the office but also marveled at how much less frequently she fought with her roommates. And that's a win for everyone.

> **Pro Tip:** Set a fixed wake-time. Getting out of bed at the same time every day—or within a margin of thirty minutes—has truly transformed so many of my patients' sleep quality. Sticking to a fixed wake-time can help you fall asleep more easily, enjoy deeper sleep, and wake up in the middle of the night less often.[8] Go ahead and entice yourself to maintain this habit with a reward like a special cup of coffee or morning shower ritual.

Exercise

Yes, I know. We've all been hearing about the importance of regular physical activity since elementary school. But before you skip this section, did you realize that exercising gives you the most bang for your buck when it comes to beating burnout? As noted in their *New York Times* bestselling book *Burnout: The Secret to Unlocking the Stress Cycle*, Emily Nagoski, PhD, and Amelia Nagoski, DMA, point out that "physical activity—literally any movement of your body—is your first line of attack in the battle against burnout."[9] When we're in the midst of a stress response (otherwise known as "fight-or-flight"), we experience an increase in the body's stress hormones, cortisol and adrenaline.[10] Exercise is an effective way to reduce the levels of those hormones.[11] In fact, the authors of *Burnout* indicate, "Physical activity is the single most efficient strategy for completing the stress response cycle."[12] Unfortunately, chronic activation of the stress response and elevated cortisol increase your risk of numerous mental and physical health problems, including headaches, digestive issues, muscle tension and pain, weight gain, memory and focus problems, sleep problems, anxiety, and depression.[13] That's why it's crucial you prioritize daily physical activity to manage your stress and keep your cortisol in check.

Moving your body in a way that feels good to you for thirty minutes or more a day can provide what feels like a total mood and mind makeover and, in the long term, could make the difference between burning out early in your career and earning that lifetime achievement award. *I'd like to thank my sneakers and free weights! I couldn't have done it without you.*

> **Pro Tip:** One concrete way to get moving: Do a "Walk-and-Talk." Plan a call with a friend once a week and take a stroll while you catch up. If the weather is bad, you can even walk around your house! If you check your steps beforehand, you'll be surprised by how many you can rack up in a short time.

Look Forward

Dinner with friends, an evening movie, window shopping on a quaint street. Scheduling pleasant activities to look forward to—and then doing them—can make life feel more satisfying and less effortful or monotonous. Even the *anticipation* of something positive is powerful. In fact, as Shawn Achor explains in *The Happiness Advantage*, "Anticipating future rewards can actually light up the pleasure centers in your brain much as the actual reward will."[14] So reminding yourself, "I get to go to this cool concert," or "I booked a massage for after work—I can't wait!" can positively impact your thoughts, feelings, and behaviors, promoting a more balanced mindset and helping you manage stress. Imagine waking up each day looking forward to something.

What qualifies as a pleasant activity? Anything you *enjoy* doing. Sometimes my patients have a hard time coming up with something they'd enjoy doing. Maybe you do, too. Maybe you came from a high-achieving family, where you were always scheduled. Maybe you were never asked what *you* want/like to do that's not attached to achievement. Maybe it's hard for you to sit by yourself, slow down, and figure that out. That's okay! Even the smallest enjoyments can make a big difference. So if it feels overwhelming to plan pleasant activities at first, build in what I call Everyday Treats that deliver tiny bursts of pleasure throughout the day: applying lavender hand lotion, using a nice pen, reading for pleasure for just five minutes in the morning, even eating a square or two of that dark chocolate again—oh my! It all helps to improve your outlook and mitigate burnout. Ideally, you'll work up to integrating both Everyday Treats and pleasant activities throughout your week, but this is a great place to start.

> **Pro Tip:** Make sure these activities are *actually* pleasant. High achievers tend to gravitate toward what's productive instead. Because our aim is to give you something to look forward to, the activity needs to be something that you *want* to do, not something you *need* to or *should* do. When I asked my patient Lucy what she could incorporate into her week, she said, "Well, I have been meaning to make time to vacuum." That's great—if you love to vacuum. So I encouraged her to ask herself: "Is this something I will look forward to doing?" It was a hard no on that one. "Then it's not a pleasant activity," I explained. "We want the activity to feel *doable* and *enjoyable*—not in any way stressful."

I acknowledge how hard it is, when you feel stressed and depleted, to have someone list what seems like *all* the things you need to do to feel better. That can just contribute to your tension. So, I'm here to encourage you to plan *one* concrete thing each week to look forward to. Just one.

When my patients report back after enacting this strategy, they often tell me they're surprised by the boost of energy they got just by *anticipating* something nice. It's really the buy-in, or foot in the door, they need to consider self-care in a real way.

Making time for pleasant activities will help you feel less anxious and give you more energy. Period.

TAKE ACTION

Choose at least one pleasant activity this week—make sure it's something you'll look forward to doing—write it in your calendar, commit to doing it, and then *enjoy!*

Bonus Boost: Add in at least two calendar reminders in the days leading up to the activity so you get the extra energy-boosting benefits that accompany *anticipating* what you've planned.

Fuel

When work is busy and your deadlines are looming, it can feel difficult to remember to hydrate and eat regularly, let alone choose something that's healthy for you. And yet refueling is oh so necessary—for your body *and* your mind. In an article he wrote for *Harvard Business Review*, psychologist and author of *Decoding Greatness*, Ron Friedman, PhD, said, "Food has a direct impact on our cognitive performance... Just about everything we eat is converted by our body into glucose, which provides the energy our brains need to stay alert. When we're running low on glucose, we have a tough time staying focused and our attention drifts. This explains why it's hard to concentrate on an empty stomach."[15] That's why Dr. Friedman emphasizes the benefits of eating more frequent, smaller meals. They help ensure your blood sugar doesn't drop or spike, which are both bad for your productivity. And he suggests being strategic about choosing foods that don't leave you feeling "groggy" (like high-fat meals) or with a post-sugar "slump" (like cereal and soda).

So, the ROI of consistently fueling yourself with high-quality, energy-boosting foods is substantial. After making a few healthful changes, my patient Helen noticed she had better concentration and more energy to study and ultimately did better on her final exams. And all she'd done was take time to eat some protein for breakfast (an egg and veggie omelet or a protein shake) and pack some nutritious snacks like walnuts, berries, and sliced apples with almond butter in her tote bag. Her healthy actions even inspired some of her friends and fellow classmates to start self-caring it up, as well.

> **Pro Tip:** Remember to refuel your mind with peaceful moments, as well. Making time for quiet during the day allows your brain to rest and reenergize. Aim for at least five minutes of mental rest most days—sit or walk in silence, meditate, or do deep breathing. Or simply sit or walk in nature. You'll still have thoughts passing through your mind—and that's fine. Just sit with nothing to prove, judge, produce, or evaluate.

Keeping both your body and mind fueled will give you the energy necessary to accomplish your current—and future—dreams and goals!

• • •

When I consider implementing S.E.L.F., I often think of my patient Agnes, who was in her late twenties and worked at a nonprofit.

I will never forget when, at the end of one session, I asked her: "Is there anything else you want to discuss before we go?"

And Agnes, overwhelmed by a never-ending to-do list, looked up at me with pleading eyes and responded, "How do I get through the rest of my day?"

Wow. In that moment, I realized just how intensely Agnes was struggling with burnout from her job. And that heart-wrenching question became pivotal for me in my recognition of high achievers' hurdles. Her dysfunctional work environment, consistent lack of anything fun or relaxing in her week, and chronic sleep problems had left her drained and running on fumes. It was time for us to pivot from discussing higher-level cognitive concepts to focusing on concrete behavioral skills she could use to feel better—*right away.*

IN THE MOMENT AND OVERWHELMED? DO THIS!

We've been hard at work, identifying long-term strategies to combat anxiety. But there are times when you need to target stress in the moment, especially when that worry is getting in the way of your productivity, calm, and ability to face the day.

These are some trusted tactics to use as needed. While they may seem simple, they *really* work. And you might be surprised how hard it can be to remember them at the height of your workday stress. So the next time you feel overwhelm mounting:

1. **Take three deep breaths.** Notice the rise and fall of your belly as you slowly inhale through your nose and exhale through your mouth. This will help provide some stress relief and reduce tension.[16]
2. **Write a list!** Grab a piece of paper and a pen—or the Notes app on your phone—and jot down your to-dos. It will help you immediately redirect your attention to a concrete, useful activity, instead of fixating on feelings of overwhelm. And it will promote an increased sense of control, focus, and calm.[17] Then, ask yourself: What *needs* to be done? Identify which task is the most important to complete. Accept that you might not be able to get everything done today. You'll improve your peace and productivity when you have a strategic plan.

3. **Quiet the noise.** Focus on completing one thing at a time. Research shows that monotasking is much more effective than multitasking, as our brains are wired for singular focus. Toggling our attention makes us inefficient and more prone to mistakes, especially if the tasks are complex.[18] Minimize distractions while you're working. Silence your phone, stay off social media, avoid anything that will disrupt your attention.
4. **Control the controllables.** Use self-care and self-talk as support. Check in with yourself: Do you need water? Food? A few minutes to move your body or hit the bathroom before you approach what's next? Watch where you choose to shine your flashlight—use short, helpful self-talk statements to keep moving forward. Remind yourself: You got this!
5. **Plan a pleasant activity.** Come up with one specific reward you can look forward to at the end of your day, whether it's hanging with a friend or watching an episode of a show you've been bingeing. Give yourself a light at the end of the tunnel!

Before Agnes left my office, as she sat across from me, I guided her through a few deep breaths and encouraged her to focus on extending her exhales.

I reassured her, "You will get through this challenging moment. You're overwhelmed, but you really are okay."

Once she was a bit calmer, we generated a self-care game plan for the rest of her day: She'd walk the long way back to work through the park to stretch her legs, see the freshly bloomed flowers, and stop to grab her favorite iced tea from a nearby café. For when she arrived back at her office, I helped her strategically prioritize the tasks she deemed most important to accomplish, one by one. And she also planned to reach out and chat with a friend that night.

Agnes was motivated to try anything to feel better and get back to her usual, productive self. Things had gotten bad enough that she was ready to make a change. Over the next few months, she began to build additional self-care practices into her daily routine, including getting back to her favorite creative hobbies and planning regular meetups with friends, determined to defeat burnout.

TAKE ACTION

Just when you thought it was a purely mental game: High achievers often manifest burnout in physical ways, too. *The party never ends!* My patients routinely suffer from the following aches and pains. Do you? Here are some curated self-care practices to help you target those issues. Choose one and try it today!

Chronically tense muscles. Perhaps you're clenching your jaw, your shoulders are scrunched up to your ears, or your neck and shoulders feel stiff and sore. To triumph over tense muscles:

- Get up and stretch in five-minute increments throughout the day. It's critical to make time for movement. Prolonged sitting is hazardous!
- Schedule a massage or take an Epsom salt bath[19] at least once a month.
- Check your posture regularly—sit or stand up straight if you notice you are slouching. Also, make sure you position your computer screen at eye level to prevent neck strain that can occur if you are looking down.[20]
- Practice tensing and then relaxing your muscles. Progressive Muscle Relaxation (PMR) can help you learn to notice when your muscle tension is triggered and how to effectively release it. This powerful tension buster can also promote

better sleep.[21] You can access a guided PMR practice on meditation apps like Headspace or Calm.
- Go for a walk at least once a day.
- "Shake It Off!" Get up and dance to at least one song. Literally shake out the stress and tension from your body. It's effective—and a good time!

Holding your breath or shallow breathing. Do you find yourself holding your breath, sighing, taking audible gasps for air or shorter, shallow breaths in your chest? That's probably your anxiety again! To breathe easier and enhance relaxation:

- Increase your awareness about your breathing. Take a beat to check if you're holding your breath at various intervals throughout the day.
- Sing. Belt out some of your favorite songs in the shower—or wherever you can—every day. Expand your lung capacity, practice regulating your breathing, and enjoy the added bonus: a mood boost.
- Schedule a laugh. I know at first this may sound hokey. I can just see those doubtful expressions! But truly, laughter is a great stress relief and can also benefit lung health.[22] So at least once a day, watch a funny video, read something humorous, or listen to a witty podcast. If you're worried you'll go down a rabbit hole and lose time, set an alarm for just five minutes and get back to work.
- Practice belly breathing (also called diaphragmatic breathing) every day to engage your diaphragm so you can inhale more air into your lungs.[23] Here are a few simple steps:

1. Sitting in a comfortable position, put one hand on your chest and one hand on your abdomen.

2. Take a slow, deep breath in through your nose, allowing the air to move down toward your abdomen. Notice your abdomen expand and feel the hand on your abdomen rise.
3. Slowly exhale through your mouth. Notice your abdomen fall and your hand move in toward your body as you breathe out.
4. Start by practicing the above sequence a few times, once a day. Slowly increase to five to ten minutes, one to four times every day.

KEEP IT DOABLE

Your days are busy. That's an understatement. So as we discussed, you are going to have to *make* time for self-care. Just like you make time for your most important meetings. This may feel challenging at first. You're likely in the habit of prioritizing basically everything else (work, classes, events, activities, friends) before your well-being. So how can you make time to create stellar, sustainable habits and become the self-care superstar you have the power to be? By keeping it doable.

As you know, setting goals that are actually achievable is vital to freeing yourself from the snare of perfectionism. And it's a must for sustaining a self-care practice long term. Since consistent self-care is what will help you overcome anxiety, defeat exhaustion, experience enduring high achievement, and live with excellence, that's kind of an important thing. So how do you keep self-care doable? Three ways: Streamline Your Options, Calendar It, and Stay Flexible.

Streamline Your Options

Decision fatigue is real! This is a rampant, if not at all surprising, issue: It's estimated that the average American adult makes a whopping thirty-five thousand decisions a day.[24] Yet research shows that our ability to make choices is negatively impacted by repeated acts of decision-making.[25] As John Tierney, coauthor of *Willpower:*

Rediscovering the Greatest Human Strength, put it so well: "No matter how rational and high-minded you try to be, you can't make decision after decision without paying a biological price. It's different from ordinary physical fatigue—you're not consciously aware of being tired—but you're low on mental energy."[26] In other words, you may notice that the more choices you make throughout the day, the harder it will be to make high-quality choices, which can adversely impact your behaviors and your trajectory.

Decision fatigue is a common obstacle when it comes to self-care. After all, part of self-care is really preserving your energy so you can strategically use that energy in ways that you want. So you're even less likely to make the time—to exercise, eat healthy, wake up at the same hour, take a walk, and more—if you have to spend extra minutes parsing out the details in real time. Instead, exhaustion over making choices often causes you to default to one of four behaviors: You put off the decision (procrastination); you make a decision without thinking things through (impulsivity); you sidestep making a decision at all (avoidance); or you bounce between choices (indecision).[27] So, minimizing decision fatigue is in itself an act of self-care, creating less stress in your life. Streamlining your options can help lessen the number of decisions you make each day so you are more able to make the best choices possible when it comes to taking care of yourself. For example, when a patient is faced with an overwhelming to-do list, I often encourage them to "Eat the Frog," which means get the thing done that you *need* to get done first, especially if you don't want to do it. (This concept, which I first encountered in one of my psych classes, is based on a quotation sometimes attributed to Mark Twain: "If it's your job to eat a frog, it's best to do it first thing in the morning. And if it's your job to eat two frogs, it's best to eat the biggest one first.") Of course, if you're working on a long-term project, such as your dissertation or a major paper, Eating the Frog could mean blocking off an hour or so (whatever feels doable) in the morning when you're freshest and focusing on just *one aspect* of that project. I'll often say,

"Where's the frog on your to-do list today?" Do that first and then the rest of the day will seem easier!

> **Pro Tip:** One element of my life that I streamline as an act of self-care is my wardrobe. It reduces the stress of daily decision-making. I wear a variation on the same outfit every single day to the office: a cashmere cardigan over a white top, black slacks, and ballet flats. That's one thing I never have to waste energy over. Dinner is another good area for streamlining. Establish three to five healthy, easy options for meals and keep those ingredients or items on hand or the take-out number on speed dial. It'll free up many minutes every night and likely lead to much healthier food choices. It helps life feel more manageable, especially during super-busy workweeks. Another hack: Agree on standing meetup times for everything from book clubs to game nights to avoid having to schedule each time. Truly, the secret to sustainable self-care is to make it as easy and convenient as possible.

Calendar It

Schedule self-care habits into your life like you would any other appointment. This will ensure that you plan for and honor the time you set aside. Schedule gym workouts, get-togethers with friends, and at least fifteen-minute lunch breaks during your workday. I strategically set an alert for one day before and also one hour before my major self-care appointments. I encourage my patients to do the same. You can still be spontaneous, but at least you'll have some planned healthy activities in place.

The most challenging kind of self-care to schedule is time off. Are you feeling lazy and uncomfortable just at the mention of it? Well, respectfully, you're not lazy at all. You work really hard. You care so much about what you want to achieve. And it's not healthy for you or anyone else to always be "on." Your brain and body need time off to recharge and replenish.

Taking time off doesn't make you lazy; it makes you *strategic*.[28] According to "How Taking a Vacation Improves Your Well-Being," a *Harvard Business Review* article by Rebecca Zucker, "An Ernst & Young study showed that for every additional 10 hours of vacation time that employees took, their year-end performance improved 8%, and another study showed that using all of your vacation time increases your chances of getting a promotion or a raise."[29]

Star players don't play the whole game. They come out to rest and Gatorade up so they can go back out on the field or court and crush it. Do the same in your professional life: Plan rest breaks. Every so often, take a longer lunch break and detach from the constant emails or texts—and de-stress for a bit. Schedule a whole day off for yourself. Or plan a vacation to somewhere you've always wanted to visit. Build in whatever time you can to refuel. And don't wait until you're already overwhelmed and feel like you need a reprieve or you'll collapse. Schedule it thoughtfully! This is critical to sustainable success.

TAKE ACTION

Take the "Post-it Note Challenge." Look at your to-do list for today. How many tasks are you trying to complete? How many small errands are you trying to squeeze into your day? Choose at least one item from your to-do list and give yourself permission *not* to do it today.

Then, write the activities that really *need* to be accomplished today, versus everything you're trying to get done, on a Post-it Note. The standard three-by-three size helps us manage our expectations of what actually has to get done versus what we'd like to get done. If you can't fit today's to-dos on your Post-it, then reevaluate how much you're trying to do in one day. It's about prioritizing and knowing it's okay not to do it all today. Pressure-Cooker, All-or-Nothing Thinking erroneously tries to make you believe that if you don't finish everything in one day, then you failed. But that distorted self-talk will just lead to you being overextended and stressed.

Bonus Boost: Look at your Post-it Note again—does it include a self-care activity? A walk after lunch? A meetup or phone chat with a friend to look forward to? If not, consider building some self-care into your day. You deserve it.

Stay Flexible

High achievers like to, yep, high achieve. So, they often believe that even self-care has to be big or it doesn't count. They train for marathons, lift the heaviest weights, or take an advanced barre class six days a week to "win" self-care. Even in this arena, the Comparison Trap rears its ugly head. And if they miss a day or decide they really don't like what they signed up for? They give up entirely or end up feeling bad about themselves for not measuring up. That's not self-care—that's All-or-Nothing Thinking. *I either do all of it or nothing at all.*

One of the best ways to keep things doable—and prevent the perfectionist unhelpful thinking—is to stay flexible. The more rigid we are in our definition of self-care and our self-talk about our habits, the less likely we'll be to keep prioritizing healthy behavior.

I speak from personal experience: Several years ago, a running coach encouraged me to slow down and not worry as much about how fast I was going. He said practicing "gentle tenacity" would keep me from injuring myself. Now I tell my patients the same thing. Exercise is important, and so we need to prioritize staying flexible—like not trying to increase both mileage and speed simultaneously!—to keep ourselves from getting hurt. Gentle tenacity helps us keep our balance. The more we insist on self-care perfection, the less we're able to achieve self-care excellence.

It needs to be okay to pivot or do less or more on a given day. Staying open helps us problem-solve and adapt our self-care goals when necessary. I like to remind my patients that life will ebb and flow; our schedules change and that's normal. During the process of implementing self-care, my clients are often really hard on themselves when they suddenly have a high-priority project and need to put extra hours in at work. "I was doing so well," they say. "Dr. A, what's wrong with me?" Here's the thing: You'll invariably have times when using healthy self-talk and self-care feel easier and times when they feel almost impossible. When things get hard, shift your focus to what feels doable, which may be less than at other moments. That's okay! You may not always be able to fit in that forty-five-minute Peloton workout you planned; sometimes it's snowed too much for you to do your usual three-mile run before work. That doesn't mean you've "ruined" your self-care streak. Doing something, rather than nothing, will make you feel better. Just remember: Done is better than perfect. So do the best you can get done. And, yes, even a five-minute workout or walk "counts." Even using the stairs instead of an elevator. Everything counts.

There is no hierarchy when it comes to taking care of yourself. If micro-moments of self-care feel good and are sustainable, go with that. Go hit a bucket of balls at the driving range, listen to your favorite music, spend extra time with your pet, slide on a pair of comfy socks, paint, write, or do whatever type of creative activity you enjoy—even buy yourself an affordable luxury like a bouquet of flowers, a new book, or some lip balm. These actions may seem basic, but their positive effects add up to a less anxious, fuller life.

BUILD IN WIGGLE ROOM

Self-care can also simply be about creating space in your schedule, instead of putting yourself in back-to-back meetings or racing to answer emails. How often do you finish a day and realize you don't even know where it went? Do you remember what you ate for lunch?

Did you even make time to eat lunch? The day is over and yet you feel like you had no time. You were buried in your work. Every minute of your day was booked solid.

Feeling the chronic pressure of *I have to get there, I can't be late, I don't have enough time* is tremendously unhealthy for your mood and overall well-being. Rushing makes it harder to think, feel, or act in balanced ways. It amplifies your anxiety and depletes your energy. In other words, it's unsustainable. Thich Nhat Hanh, the revered Buddhist monk who was nominated for the Nobel Peace Prize by Martin Luther King Jr., said it so well: "We will be more successful in all our endeavors if we can let go of the habit of running all the time, and take little pauses to relax and re-center ourselves. And we'll also have a lot more joy in living."

Think of how nice it feels when someone says to you, "No rush. Take your time." And really means it. Give yourself that gift of a second to de-stress by building wiggle room into your calendar. It means giving yourself extra time between tasks to stop and take a few breaths instead of barraging your brain with constant problems to solve. When you allow yourself a little wiggle room, your fast pace can slow, which is often when you generate some of your best ideas. Taking a little extra time to sit and sip your morning tea or coffee and stare out the window, or choosing the more scenic, winding route rather than seeking shortcuts for speed, can inspire innovation.

The simplest self-care starts by creating enough wiggle room to be aware of the moment you are in.

You deserve to start seeing the spaces between activities. They're fuel for the mind and body, like a long, slow exhale.

SELF-TALK FOR SUSTAINING SELF-CARE

Of course, if you don't really *believe* that self-care is important, you won't make time for it. That's why it's crucial that you optimize your self-talk so you can continually acknowledge the positive impact your self-care has on your mood, health, and overall functioning. Whenever you make time for a moment of calm or pleasure, give yourself credit. Yes! I'm talking to you! Tell yourself, "I'm glad I did that. Good work!," or "High five from Dr. A!" and recognize how the self-care helped you. Maybe what you did decreased your anxiety, improved or promoted your physical health and well-being, helped you laugh and relax, or increased your energy so you could be more creative, productive, or effective in your work or interpersonal interactions. By taking time to notice the benefits of self-care, you increase the likelihood that you'll keep the habits up.

Here are some self-talk pivots that can help you transform self-sabotaging thoughts into success-promoting ones. Changing how you *think* about self-care can help you *feel* more motivated so you'll implement more self-care *behaviors* to energize and fuel yourself forward toward sustainable excellence. As always, I encourage you to choose the self-talk phrases that feel most believable to you—the ones that resonate will be the ones that help the most:

SELF-TALK PIVOTS

Self-Sabotaging	Success-Promoting
"Self-care is a waste of time."	"Self-care boosts my mood and energy."
	"Self-care makes me more productive."
	"Self-care will accelerate my success."
"I shouldn't need self-care."	"Self-care is necessary for every human."
	"Self-care is strategic."
	"Self-care will help me be my best."

Self-Sabotaging	Success-Promoting
"I just lost twenty minutes going for that walk."	"I just gave myself a brain reboot." "I just gave myself an energy boost." "My creativity is flowing."
"Self-care is selfish."	"I deserve to take good care of myself." "Taking care of myself lets me show up for others." "Self-care has a positive ripple effect."
"It's too much effort to make social plans."	"I love having plans to look forward to." "It's important to have something fun to anticipate." "Start small. Self-care can be doable!"
"Just an hour more, then I'll stop."	"I'll be more on point tomorrow if I'm rested." "I need fuel in my system to go full speed." "A short break will give me a second wind."
"I should be doing work."	"Making time for exercise keeps me strong." "Pausing to breathe deeply helps me feel calm." "Self-care is worth the time."

Feeling reenergized? Now that you've begun to implement a *doable* self-care practice, next up—perhaps after a short break!—we'll tackle how to turn your worry into wonder.

TOP TAKEAWAYS

- Self-care is not self-indulgent—it's necessary and strategic.
- Even the *anticipation* of something positive is powerful.
- You deserve to take good care of yourself. Practice gentle tenacity.
- Schedule self-care into your calendar. Embrace wiggle room. Enjoy sustainable success.
- Eat the Frog! Tackle what you're dreading first.
- How many items are on your Post-it Note to-do list today?

ESSENTIAL #3

NAVIGATE UNCERTAINTY WITH CURIOSITY

Wisdom begins in wonder.

—Socrates

There is no such thing as a life without uncertainty. As convenient as it might be to walk into every situation with full confidence about the outcome, the reality is that our existence is filled with unknowns, no matter how much we try to plan and eliminate possible surprises. The future is inherently uncharted. Will we get the job, the promotion, the raise? Will the date go well? Will the audience or publication or professor be receptive? Will he text me back? Will the weather hold? More often than not, we must approach even high-stakes situations unsure of what complicating—or serendipitous!—curveballs might be thrown into the mix. And as a result, there is no avoiding uncertainty. There is only learning to sit with it so that it doesn't cause excessive discomfort and stress in our lives or hamper our success.

Easier said than done, especially for high achievers, who prefer concrete answers and predictable plans and are laser-focused on outcomes. I can tell you a thousand times to "enjoy the process," but that's a tall order if you're feeling panicked. We need to first explore why uncertainty feels so challenging, then identify the cognitive distortions that assail you in those instances, and finally equip you with science-based strategies to effectively navigate ambiguity.

WHY DOES UNCERTAINTY FEEL SO HARD?

When faced with uncertainty, the human brain is hardwired to predict negative outcomes. Evolutionarily, this *negativity bias* has helped humans make essential life-or-death decisions. The brain doesn't wait to decide whether that rustle in the bushes is a threat or just the wind. It acts immediately to keep us safe. That's because, as psychologist and *New York Times* bestselling author Dr. Rick Hanson points out in his book *Hardwiring Happiness*, "Rule #1 in the wild is: Eat lunch today—don't *be* lunch today." He explains that while the negativity bias "emerged in harsh settings very different from our own, it continues to operate inside us today as we drive in traffic, head into a meeting, settle a sibling squabble, try to diet, watch the news, juggle housework, pay bills, or go on a date. Your brain has a hair-trigger readiness to go negative to help you survive."[1]

How can we help but assume the worst?

There is one way this may impact your life on a regular basis: the "Sunday Scaries." My high-achieving patients regularly report that their workweek anxiety begins to ramp up as Saturday turns to Sunday, and crescendos into panic—about looming to-do lists, deadlines, or classes—as the sun sets on the weekend.

In addition to those feelings of uncontrollable anxiety or dread, perhaps you've also experienced physical symptoms like tense muscles, stomach distress, and difficulty falling and staying asleep. That's your body's natural fight-or-flight reaction to danger (that burst of cortisol and adrenaline in response to stress that we talked about), which dates back to a time when we relied on it for survival—readying you for whatever is rustling in the bushes! And that ancient instinct so plagues my patients on Sundays that I began referring to what looms as Woolly Mammoth Mondays. Unfortunately, the human brain doesn't distinguish between the stress of needing to present at your Monday morning all-hands meeting and a woolly mammoth approaching you head-on as a cave person. So once you start spinning about what's coming and how you "need it to go well," your fight-or-flight kicks in. High levels of anxiety can occur when nothing bad has even happened.

You may have experienced this *anticipatory anxiety* when negotiating a higher salary, awaiting news about a grant proposal or article you submitted, launching a product, or starting a new job. As a high achiever, you're likely not a fan of waiting patiently to see what happens next.

I often ask my patients, "When is your anxiety the worst: before you give your presentation, during your presentation, or after it's over?" "Before" is the nearly unanimous answer. When you're alone with your thoughts, waiting to go on, that's often when worry, self-doubt, and all those pernicious cognitive distortions find their way into your cerebral space and make you believe: "I can't do this. Why did I think I could? I'm going to crash and burn."

JUMPING TO CONCLUSIONS...AGAIN

Oh, hello, cognitive distortion! We're back to Jumping to Conclusions, that pesky member of the Troublesome Trifecta, the unhelpful thought patterns that most often hinder high achievers. It's that unbalanced way we have of dealing with uncertainty by making assumptions about what will happen or what someone thinks about us.

Well, it's back. On Sunday or any day when we're approaching something we're nervous about or when the outcome is unknown.

When in doubt and stressed out about the future, we tend to assume the worst. We think, "The workweek will be terrible! I'm exhausted in advance. I'll never get everything done! My coworkers are going to be annoying! My boss is going to choose someone else for that upcoming project!" In short, Woolly Mammoth Monday is going to suck.

Not exactly helpful—or motivational—self-talk to prepare us for a winning week.

As a reminder, there are two standard ways we jump to conclusions. The first is Negative Fortune-Telling, when we gaze into the hazy depth of our crystal ball and predict a forecast of gloom and more gloom. This is the belief that some upcoming situation or circumstance is doomed to fail, though it hasn't happened yet. For example, my patient Wilson's job was contingent on him passing the bar exam. The closer it got to test day, the more anxious he felt—and the more convinced he became that he was going to fail.

Confronted with uncertainty, he was mired in worry, which did not empower him to succeed or motivate him to study. Conversely, his unhelpful thoughts impacted his behaviors, and he fell into anticipatory paralysis. This subversive soothsaying became a self-fulfilling prophecy. Approaching the future with fear and negative assumptions zapped his energy, made him feel defeated in advance, and stopped him in his tracks.

The second way we jump to conclusions? Mind Reading! You know, that's when you assume that a coworker, boss, interviewer, or attractive somebody sitting across from you doesn't like you or is responding negatively to you without any evidence to that effect.

Frequently, this occurs when we are invested in what someone else thinks or feels about us and our worries hijack our capacity to perceive the situation objectively. In reality, it's impossible to be certain what's happening in someone else's head, so your worry makes you jump to the worst possible conclusions.

It may feel self-protective to imagine the worst in hopes of getting ahead of any negative opinions or outcomes, but actually it erodes your calm and confidence and sets the stage for unfortunate interactions. Take my client Tom, who arrived at the office early one morning and was sipping his coffee and prepping for his day when his boss showed up. Usually, she greeted him warmly, but this morning she walked right by with barely a nod. Uncertain of her motivations, Tom instantly began stressing: "She must be mad at me!"

How do you think he felt as a result of Jumping to Conclusions? You guessed it: concerned, tense, insecure. For the rest of the day, he struggled to concentrate. At his afternoon meeting, he didn't dare speak up for fear of misstepping. So, Mind Reading actually hindered his productivity and professional collaboration.

REMEMBER YOUR PROBLEM-SOLVING PROWESS!

The writing is on the wall: When the future feels frightening, letting our worries take over can only stymie us on the path to sustainable achievement. Worry undermines our ability to handle what arises, and it's ultimately about a lack of confidence in our own capacity to overcome challenges.

Ironically, high achievers are almost always incredible problem-solvers. Yes, you! And yet when insecurity creeps in and we start to feel uncertain, we often distrust our ability to manage what comes our way. We forget that, while we have to sit with uncertainty, we still have agency! For example, my patients frequently grapple with anxiety around stomach issues, worrying that they might not feel well during a big meeting or event. But what is the likelihood that there is no bathroom available? Couldn't you locate one beforehand, just in case, so you have a plan? What is the likelihood that, should the situation truly become an emergency, you won't make it in time? That there aren't stomach medications, or even calming teas or foods, that you could rely on in advance to mitigate those issues? Conversely, what are the odds that, like the myriad work crises that cross your desk, you *might* be able to handle this?

When the worry takes over, confidence in our problem-solving abilities seems to go out the window. Staying curious can help. Once, years ago, I was at the airport renting a car—a convertible!—in Florida en route to an interview for a job I really wanted. While finishing up the rental paperwork, I found myself feeling nervous. I started peppering the sales associate with questions: "Once I get out of this office, how will I find the right car? Then how do I get out of the airport?" and on from there. Finally, she looked at me and said thoughtfully, "When you step outside this building, you'll know where to go. There are going to be signs. It's going to be okay. You just need to *go*." That interaction has always stayed with me. In that moment, distracted by baseline nerves about an important opportunity, I wasn't trusting my own ability to problem-solve. The woman's point was literal but also poignant: Once we step outside the box of our own heads and look around, our perspective is much clearer.

We've got this, whether everything is mapped out for us or not. We want a lighthouse that illuminates the whole path, but instead we usually get a lantern that reveals a bit at a time. So we need to ask ourselves: "Am I minimizing my strengths by forgetting I'm a good problem-solver? Forgetting my own agency?" There are always unknowns. But we've got to trust that, with that lantern glow and our problem-solving skills, we're going to be just fine. And once we trust ourselves to take action and follow our curiosity to solutions, we usually feel empowered or inspired instead of scared.

STAYING CURIOUS

Fortunately, all is not lost. Because, at the heart of problem-solving lies curiosity or "a strong desire to know or learn something."[2] And curiosity is the ideal alternative to panicking in the face of uncertainty. Staying curious will help you move from worrying about the *what if*s in life to focusing on *what is* and wondering about what's possible. Because if you can stop fearing the future and instead turn moments of uncertainty into possibilities for growth and expansion, for learning new skills that can only benefit your success, then you can lessen that unpleasant and debilitating worry. When you do that, you'll be able to face the ambiguities of life without draining your battery.

Say my patient Tom's boss ignored him and, instead of spiraling into anxiety, he chose to stay curious. What if, as opposed to assuming she was angry, he wondered what might be causing her uncharacteristic behavior? After all, one reason Mind Reading is so unhelpful is that we never know what another person might be coping with in their own life. What if, instead of getting stressed, Tom took a moment later to ask his boss how she was doing? Imagine how much better he—and even possibly she—might feel. Staying curious would help him optimally navigate the situation instead of amp up his anxiety. Goodbye worry, hello productivity!

3 BENEFITS OF STAYING CURIOUS

Staying curious is a fantastic—dare I say, *excellent*—alternative to Jumping to Conclusions. In fact, it's the basis for overcoming our fears of uncertainty, overall. Staying curious helps us:

1. **Problem-solve.** As we established, when we get out of our own way, we high achievers can seek solutions with the best of them.
2. **Protect our energy.** Here's the thing: Worrying is exhausting. So staying curious is a kind of self-care—it optimizes our mental energy and channels our attention on the present moment and on what we can control, so we show up fully engaged.
3. **Prevent needless suffering and suffering twice.** Needless suffering is worrying about something that hasn't happened yet, which ultimately either goes better than you imagined or doesn't happen at all. Suffering twice is when you convince yourself that something won't go well and are right. It's true. Sometimes

difficult things happen. Even so, you don't do yourself any favors by suffering in your Negative Fortune-Telling imagination *and* in reality. Instead, stay curious to focus on *what is* rather than *what if* and remember that all you can do is wait and see. If the outcome isn't positive, you can cross that bridge when you come to it.

ACKNOWLEDGING AMBIGUITY

Okay, curiosity sounds great and all, but in the face of the unknown, how do you shift from deep discomfort into a desire to learn? After all, as a high achiever, you're ambitious, you set big goals, and you want to achieve them, which makes you tremendously attached to the end result over the process. Sitting with the possibility that things won't work out the way you want is bound to make you anxious.

As is so often the case, the first step is admitting you have a problem. Unless you accept that life is inherently unpredictable and learn to tolerate the discomfort of not knowing, you will be more prone to distorted thinking and, thus, anxiety. And no one wants that. Indeed, I often tell patients: Ambiguous situations are ripe for cognitive distortions. There are some things you just *can't* know. Uncertainty exists.

You do not need to like this. Honestly, I don't always like it! It's scary. But there is so much power in sitting with it.

So identify when there's ambiguity, rather than avoiding, resisting, or denying its existence. Name the source of what's making you feel anxious to begin to stop the spin and bring higher-level functioning to the forefront. Acknowledging that ambiguity can simply mean saying to yourself, "I don't have all of the information right now," or "I can't know for sure what that person thinks or what will happen." Doing this will help you be less likely to jump to conclusions and begin a worry spiral.

If you're feeling stressed or defeated in advance of a situation, ask yourself: Is there something in my life right now that's making me fall into distortions like Negative Fortune-Telling or Mind Reading?

Are you trying something new? Waiting for results? Socializing more? Attending an upcoming industry conference? In the categories of home, health, and work, do you have anything going on that you're anticipating?

If so, name it to raise awareness about how you might be Jumping to Conclusions. Acknowledge the ambiguity, whatever that might be!

Once you identify that uncertainty, we can begin to use strategies to ameliorate your anxiety. Let's exhale. And now you're ready to learn four cognitive strategies for staying curious instead of stressed out: Worry to Wonder, Poke Holes, Play It Out, and Predict Neutral.

From Worry to Wonder

As American humorist Erma Bombeck once said, "Worry is like a rocking chair: It gives you something to do but never gets you anywhere." It focuses on future unknowns—without anything actionable. It spotlights what you *don't* want to happen but doesn't move you toward things you do want.

Have you ever thought: "What if it doesn't go well? What if they meet me and don't like me? What if I don't get invited into the company, or university, or group that I want? What if I never achieve this goal? What if I sound like a total idiot? What if I just can't handle it?"

These what-ifs might sound like questions, but in fact they're more like foregone conclusions, spurring Negative Fortune-Telling and Mind Reading. By the time my patients start asking themselves, "What if...?" I know they're already on their way down the worry rabbit hole. Take Kavita, my client who was up for a promotion that was tied to a big project she was overseeing. "What if the project doesn't go well, Dr. A?" she worried. "Then I definitely won't get the promotion. And I'll have to tell everyone I didn't get it. They'll think I can't handle things at work. That I'm not good enough." Clouded by negative assumptions, she began worrying about work from morning till night.

Catching your what-ifs is one powerful way to mitigate worry and turn it to wonder. If worry is thinking about the future with fear, then wonder is thinking about the future with curiosity, which, as you recall, is propelled by a desire to discover. When faced with uncertainty, you might as well figure out what you could learn. This might sound like: "I wonder how it will go? I wonder what it'll be like? I wonder who will be there? I wonder what will come out of this? I wonder who I could ask about this?"

During times of unknowing, choosing to wonder rather than worry means waiting to *see what actually happens* and *asking questions* to learn more, just like my client Tom could directly ask his boss how she was doing to find out what she was *actually* thinking instead of making assumptions. Wonder allows you to stay curious to better navigate ambiguous situations—a powerful advantage.[3] Instead of stressing that you won't pass your licensing exam, what if you wonder what might be on the test or ask questions about how to best prepare for it? You'll be more likely to schedule in study time, review important material, or meet with a study group or tutor, which will help you do well. Cultivating wonder can help you make progress rather than get stuck in panic.

> **Pro Tip:** Convert worry into wonder by strategically shifting your self-talk: Anytime you notice yourself thinking, "What if...?" practice saying, "I wonder..." instead.

Poke Holes

Wondering isn't the only way to transform our worry in the face of uncertainty. Using some of our existing tools, we can also improve our self-talk by poking holes in unbalanced thoughts. We're getting to be pros at that, right?

It's true that people rarely predict positive outcomes because of that negativity bias we discussed. When was the last time you thought to yourself: "This is going to go great!" or "I really think they're going to like me for who I am!" Nope, we humans tend to think more about negative, unpleasant, or unwanted outcomes in uncertain situations because we are so loss averse.

Though it's inherently illusory, we often try to protect ourselves from possible disappointment and let ourselves off the hook by predicting that things will go poorly. In truth, we'll feel upset about losing out on that fellowship, job, or relationship, regardless. The only thing we'll be blunting is the opportunity to feel the good things—hope, excitement, and, *yes*, curiosity!

The solution is not about putting on rose-colored glasses. In fact, if anything, I'd like you to take all glasses off. My goal is to help you see your situation as it is, without any negative or positive filters. To stick to the facts, not feelings that have morphed into false realities in your mind. Don't let those cognitive distortions bully you into believing non-evidence-based predictions that bad things will definitely occur! But how do you overcome them?

Poke Holes! Begin by asking: "How is my thought *not necessarily true*?"

When it comes to Negative Fortune-Telling, the answer is pretty clear. Any negative thought about what will happen in the future is not necessarily true because *the future hasn't happened yet*. Even if there have been times when you accurately anticipated an outcome, no prediction is definitive. That's the ace up your sleeve. So whenever you want to poke a serious hole in your unhelpful fortune-telling distortion, remind yourself: "This hasn't happened yet."

Since there's no way of knowing what other people are thinking, no matter how good you believe you are at reading people or how well you know someone, your Mind Reading thoughts are also *not necessarily* true. Remind yourself: "I can't know for sure what someone thinks unless they tell me (and they tell the truth!)."

Once you've answered that initial question, delve even deeper. Ask yourself:

- **Am I making assumptions?** Is my thought a prediction about something that hasn't happened? Am I only *presuming* what another person might be thinking?
- **Are there other possibilities?** Could something other than my thought happen? What are alternative interpretations or explanations for what's going on?

Play It Out

Despite all my years working with high achievers, it still fascinates me how even C-suite executives—high-powered lawyers, accomplished academicians, and others at the top of their game—doubt their own ability to effectively cope with what might happen in the future. It doesn't matter how high they rise or how many stressful situations they've managed in the past. They still suffer from fragile self-confidence.

To help them recognize their own abilities in this arena and also maintain perspective about the potential fallout, I'll say, "Let's play it out." Then I ask them to imagine what might happen if the worst-case scenario—the outcome they fear—actually became a reality. In playing it out, they realize a few essential things: First, those feared outcomes may be *possible*, but they're not *probable*. Second, even if that "failure" did come to pass, they'd be okay. They might find themselves in legitimately difficult or undesirable situations, but they would still have the ability to help themselves through it. For instance, if they were worried about what would happen if the company they founded went under or their relationship fell apart, we'd talk about how they'd lean on their network, utilize their resources, and find ways to troubleshoot, pivot, and problem-solve to keep moving forward. Lastly, I encourage them to remember that they are not alone. None of us are. We can always reach out to other people—friends, therapists, mentors, medical professionals—for much-needed support. We all need help sometimes. There's no shame in it.

> **Pro Tip:** Watch out for *possibility* versus *probability*. This can be the difference between anxiety and calm. For example, just because there's a possibility you could get fired for forgetting to attend your team's weekly check-in, that doesn't mean there's a high probability that your boss will dismiss you for one missed meeting.

Predict Neutral

Next up: Predict Neutral. This strategy is designed to help you remain unbiased and reality-based rather than negative. Concretely, it means that when you're faced with an ambiguous situation, circumstance, or interaction, you choose not to predict in a negative *or* positive direction. Instead, you stay neutral. You don't let yourself assume anything because you recognize that uncertainty exists in that moment. For example:

The Situation: Your landlord tells you they're selling the building where you live, in your highly coveted neighborhood, and you need to move out.

Negative Fortune-Telling Prediction: "Ugh, I'll never find a decent apartment I can afford in this area! I'll have to live with roommates who will probably be loud and messy or move to a less desirable part of the city."

Predict Neutral: "I'll have to set up some appointments with brokers, reach out to friends, and see what's available right now."

The Situation: You met with a philanthropist to ask her for a sizable contribution to a fundraising event you're helping to arrange.
Mind Reading Prediction: "I could tell she didn't like me. She probably thinks I don't know what I'm doing."
Predict Neutral: "She hasn't expressed how she feels about me or the event one way or the other. I can't know at this moment whether she'll make a donation."

Assume nothing and move forward.

TAKE ACTION

Now it's your turn: Think of an ambiguous situation in your life that causes you stress. Make sure it's a more minor scenario rather than something deeply important. It's ideal to practice new skills in a way that feels somewhat challenging but not overwhelming. Describe what a *before* thought might sound like if you allow your negativity bias to dictate an unhelpful, negative prediction. Next, generate an *after* thought by choosing to Predict Neutral. Notice how that shift impacts your energy and mood.

Your Situation:

Negative Fortune-Telling / Mind Reading Prediction:

Predict Neutral:

The Impact (How did you feel after you Predicted Neutral?):

LEVEL UP YOUR SELF-TALK

Now that you've tried Predicting Neutral on for size and hopefully lowered your anticipatory anxiety level, you're on the path to recognizing that, whatever the future holds, you've got what you need to handle it.

But wait! There's more, if you're up for the challenge (which you are because, well, you're a high achiever): Beyond staying neutral in moments of ambiguity, you can actually tiptoe toward the positive. To level up your self-talk, first learn self-talk phrases to Stay Curious, then Be Hopeful (yep!), and finally Get Excited.

Let's See What Happens, Come What May, Stay Curious About Uncertainty

It's one thing to wonder what might happen versus assume the worst. It's another to believe in your core that you'll figure things out and get help as needed. That's where two of my favorite phrases come in: "Let's see what happens" and "Come what may."

Adding these expressions to your repertoire can help you stay curious, the ultimate goal when navigating uncertainty. For instance, this type of balanced self-talk might sound like: "I'm worried the project won't go well, *but* it hasn't happened yet. Worrying will just waste my time. I can choose to stay curious. I'll focus on preparing and doing my best. Then, let's see what happens. Come what may, I'll know I did my best and find a way to manage what's next."

"Come what may" specifically can help you build confidence in your ability to cope with whatever happens in the future. You can remind yourself: *Come what may, I'll know I did the best I could given the circumstances. And I'll keep trying to do my best now. That's all I can do.*

When you bolster your belief in yourself and trust you will do your best no matter what the challenge—which might even mean collaborating with people or seeking help from others—you won't feel as anxious about the future. Trusting yourself is a huge relief! Remember: You are human and, although your best will differ by the day or situation, your best is enough. Excellence is enough.

Be Hopeful About Possibility

Staying curious is a big win. But what if, once you've mastered that, you could actually allow yourself to be *hopeful*? This can be a hard sell for high achievers in the midst of an anxious moment about an upcoming event. Fair enough. Yet finding a way to be hopeful in uncertain situations begins with simply asking: What might that look like?

My patient Grant, for instance, was scheduled for a second interview at a company he really liked and was nervous about doing well. "What if I say something stupid and don't get the job?" he asked, adjusting his glasses. You can imagine how that thought increased his fear and decreased the chances of him showing up as his best self. So first, we discussed staying curious about the unknown and practicing balanced self-talk: "I really want the job, but I can't know what will happen," he said. "So I'll just prepare well and do the best I can. Let's see how it goes. Come what may, I'll be alright."

Next, I encouraged Grant to consider stepping up to hopefulness. I could tell he had it in him! Tentatively, he adapted his words to be a bit more positive: "I really want the job, but I can't know for sure what will happen. I'll just prepare and do the best I can. I'm hopeful it'll go well, and I'll get the job. If I don't, I'm hopeful I'll at least have gotten some good interviewing practice and will find something else great soon."

Recognizing that uncertainty actually allows for the possibility of *good* things in the future, as well as challenges, can be a game-changer.

Get Excited About Opportunity

What if, in anticipation of the future, you could get...excited? Pull out the confetti! Maybe? I know. It's a lot to ask to see chances for growth in the face of the unknown. Yep, an even harder sell than being hopeful, whether it's about a big exam, a project, or even a first date. But it's not as impossible as it may seem. You've already learned to stay curious and be hopeful. Now, by leveling up your self-talk one more time, you can open yourself up to all the ways an uncertain situation can spell beneficial opportunities—no matter how it goes.

The truth is that, no matter how much we dread them, most situations wind up being informative, enjoyable, or both. That's not toxic positivity. It's reality. Everything we experience informs us and, at the very least, most of the time, it's not as awful as we anticipate. As ambitious people, interested largely in ascension, we need to remember that the more skills and information we amass, the more marketable we become. The less energy we waste on anxiety, the more we have to put toward our sustained success.

Remind yourself: "Come what may, I'm going to learn from this."

Let's imagine you've got a first date. If it goes fine, there's the opportunity to make a new friend. If it goes amazing, maybe you've just met the partner of your dreams! If it turns out to be a dud date, then you've gained clarity about what qualities you want or don't want in a mate, which may inform different choices next time. Maybe you got a good story out of it. Whatever happens, thinking about the date in this way helps it to become a win-win for you: You can now view it as *enjoyable* or *informative*—not a waste of time! Of course, "enjoyable" feels preferable. But "informative" experiences—especially when things don't go the way we hoped—are often where we ascertain the most about ourselves, others, and the world. Like it or not, typically we learn the most from adversity.

Having a handle on staying curious and being hopeful, Grant was game to try his hand at getting excited about his interview. "I really want this job, but I can't know what will happen," he began again. "I'll focus on preparing well and doing the best I can. I can get excited that I might be offered the job. And no matter how it goes, I'll be excited for the opportunity to hone my interview skills and meet new people."

Of course, all of Grant's pre-interview jitters didn't instantly vanish. But his new excitement-promoting self-talk—versus feeling defeated in advance—could have been the difference between him being hired or not. Regardless of whether Grant got the job (he did, by the way), his upgraded self-talk definitely lowered his level of anxiety around the interview.

So, practice training yourself to use Get Excited self-talk in ambiguous situations. It'll help decrease your worry and make whatever actually happens much easier to manage.

LEVEL UP YOUR BEHAVIORS

We've talked a lot now about how to improve our approach to the unknown using cognitive strategies (our thoughts) to get out of our own way and find sustained success, but there are some clear-cut *behavioral* solutions that can make a big difference in how we cope with uncertainty, too. As a high achiever, I think you're going to like these practical solutions.

Preparation

As poet Robert Frost noted, "The best way out is through." You have to live your way through the anxious moments. So instead of expending your energy worrying about some uncertain future result, constructively channel your attention on what you *can* control right now. And that's preparing for what's coming! Guess what: that's focusing on the process—the concrete actions within your control—instead of the outcome.

One thing I've noticed is that a lot of my high-achieving clients, especially the lawyers, get overwhelmed in advance of social or networking events because they dread small talk. So for networking gatherings, conferences, workshops, or social events, we prepare. We brainstorm topics to avoid and to steer toward, staying away from politics and religion and focusing on lighter commentary on recent books they've read or activities they enjoy. The same goes for patients who are grappling with difficult personal issues—like loss of a loved one, divorce, health issues, or a job change—that they don't particularly want to discuss. Hello, anticipatory anxiety! For them, we work to develop "stock answers" so they don't have as much of an intense emotional response in the moment. We use phrases like: "Thanks for asking. I'm making it through." Or, "It's for the best." Then redirect. Knowing what they do and don't want to talk about helps them feel more calm and confident when they're walking through those doors to the event.

So if you're nervous in anticipation of a job interview, for example, do your homework ahead of time: Research the company's culture or prepare a list of questions to ask. If you have a final coming up, create flash cards for the sections that make you the most uneasy, instead of worrying about your end-of-semester grade. Prep for your Monday morning meeting on Friday during work hours, rather than dreading it the whole weekend and frantically cramming on Sunday night when you most need to decompress. Directing your energy, time, and attention into the process of preparing for your upcoming event will tame your anticipatory anxiety, build your confidence, and give you forward momentum.

> **Pro Tip:** Remember that your energy is a finite resource. Ask yourself: Do I want to drain my battery stressing about what might happen? Or do I want to devote as much of my energy as possible to preparing for success?

Strategic Distraction

All prepared? Bring on the self-care! It's time to take a break or schedule a pleasant activity! I don't mean to distract yourself in order to *avoid* what you need to do. Not at all. Hence, *strategic* distraction. After completing your preparation, doing something intentionally to give your brain a rest and reset can help minimize needless worrying and give you somewhere else to focus your attention. When you've been working really hard to prepare for something big, your mind can become exhausted and your emotions intense. So go for a walk or hit the gym, do some yoga or meditate, get outside for some fresh air, watch a funny movie, meet up with a friend, or hang out with a pet. Do anything enjoyable to enhance your energy and take your focus off the feared forthcoming event!

TAKE ACTION

Got something big coming up? Unsure of the outcome? Ask yourself: Is there anything else I can do to prepare? If not, what are three things you could do to distract yourself that would take your mind off your worry and you would feel good about? It could be something pleasant and relaxing or even productive. Organizing your closet, doing dishes, and going grocery shopping can offer a sense of control when you're confronted with uncertainty. Come up with three ideas about how to strategically distract yourself. Make a list. Write it down!

Participation

As a kid, I learned a saying that has always stayed with me: "Don't anticipate! Participate!" The active preparation—studying, reviewing, researching, rehearsing—needs to come to an end at some point. Eventually, it's showtime! So once you've readied and taken some time to recharge your batteries, it's time to go to that meeting. Take that exam for which you've studied so diligently. Give that presentation. See how it goes. Just do it. Your cognitive distortions will deceive you into feeling anxious in anticipation. You may have thoughts like, "I'm still not ready, it's got to be perfect, I need to keep preparing!" But don't give in to that negative self-talk! Instead, take action. Remember, avoidance perpetuates anxiety; approach overcomes anxiety. And when you do finish participating, won or lost, you'll have accomplished the task!

POST-PARTICIPATION AMNESIA

"So how'd it go?" I asked my patient Daphne as she sat down on my couch, trusty four-colored Bic pen in hand and lined legal pad on my lap. I was ready to write down the update I'd been looking forward to since our previous session the week before when she was so worried about her stomach hurting during a presentation.

"Uh, how'd what go, Dr. A?" And I couldn't help but smile. Although I've heard that reply countless times, it still gives me pause. We humans are an interesting bunch. One week, our world can be consumed by a situation and feel as if it's crashing down on top of us, and then the next week, we can't even remember that anxiety-provoking predicament that was poised to ruin our lives. So I reminded her, "Remember, last week you told me you were terrified about your stomach hurting during the presentation on Friday?" Daphne paused to think, and then responded, "Oh, yeah. No, it went fine."

This Post-Participation Amnesia, as I call it, frequently occurs after anxiety-provoking events have passed, such as exams, dates, speeches, conferences, consults with doctors, or job interviews. It's as if once the feared event passes, and wasn't as bad as anticipated, patients almost completely forget about it. What was life-or-death becomes no big deal. If there's any fundamental lesson in dealing with uncertainty, that's it. Reality is rarely as frightening as the anticipation. And since the anxiety is all for naught, we might as well stay curious instead.

TOP TAKEAWAYS

- The future is inherently uncharted. There is no such thing as a life without uncertainty. Acknowledge it.
- Life gives us a lantern, not a lighthouse, to guide us toward our future.
- Come what may, you have the problem-solving skills to handle any outcome.
- In a moment of ambiguity? Stay Curious. Be Hopeful. Get Excited.
- Trust yourself. You're a high achiever. You'll find your way out of the parking lot.

ESSENTIAL #4

CULTIVATE HEALTHY CONNECTIONS

*Too often we underestimate the power of a touch,
a smile, a kind word, a listening ear, an honest
compliment, or the smallest act of caring, all of which
have the potential to turn a life around.*

—Leo Buscaglia

The first three Essentials we've discussed are about focusing on yourself—how to manage the thoughts, feelings, and behaviors that deter you, impact your energy, and increase your worry. How to approach perfectionism, overwhelm, and uncertainty—and flip them on their heads. Now it's time to explore how to skillfully manage the number one source of *external* stress for high achievers: relationships with others.

In fact, in order to truly thrive, we need to learn how to *capitalize* on the concept of connections in our lives.

"Relationships?" you may be lamenting. "On top of everything else?"

I get it. As someone who is incredibly driven, you likely prefer to put as much of your energy as possible directly toward your goals. And interpersonal connections may at first seem like a challenging distraction, especially to high achievers who sometimes feel like social demands are even more exhausting than day-to-day work pressures. But in their healthiest form, relationships—with friends, family members, and office buddies—are one of the most efficient accelerants to your success. And unfortunately, unhealthy relationships can be one of the most detrimental impediments.

So having supportive connections—as well as addressing the relationships that contribute to your anxiety and stress—is not optional if you want to make professional headway. Because unmanaged stress is the biggest obstacle to happiness and achievement for my clients. And ironically, relationships are both the greatest source of stress in our lives and also one of the most powerful stress management tools.

RELATIONSHIPS, STRESS, AND PERFORMANCE

In order to understand how important relationships are to your ability to be sustainably successful, first it's essential to learn about the fundamentals of stress management. The truth is, everyone experiences stress in their lives. So what is stress? Simply put, stress is our response to a challenge or change. And it's not always a bad thing. In fact, Dr. John D. Otis, psychologist and research associate professor at Boston University, says, "Any event that requires us to make changes and put forth effort involves a certain amount of stress."[1] In other words, stress can be related to positive events like accepting a promotion, preparing for a competition, or buying a home. So stress is a part of what gets you going in the morning, propels you to act, and inspires you to conquer ambitious objectives. It can translate into excitement and positive anticipation, especially, as Dr. Otis points out, if you think you have a good chance of succeeding. This can provide the energy and focus you need to take your game to the next level.

So it's about our *perception* of the situation or event. If we perceive that this is something we can handle and are likely to succeed at, we'll be excited, eager, and motivated. That's a healthy level of arousal or stress. Conversely, if we perceive a situation or challenge as beyond our ability to cope and tell ourselves, "I can't handle this!" we'll feel overwhelmed. And that's when stress becomes *distress*.

It's when the stress is interpreted as "too much" that high achievers experience the downside: anxiety, overwhelm, exhaustion, and burnout, all of which adversely affect a person's ability to handle what comes their way and function at the highest level.

This powerful relationship between stress and performance is explained by the Yerkes-Dodson law, which is illustrated as an inverted U shape.[2] In the diagram below, stress is referred to as "arousal." The optimal amount of stress is indicated at the top of the curve:

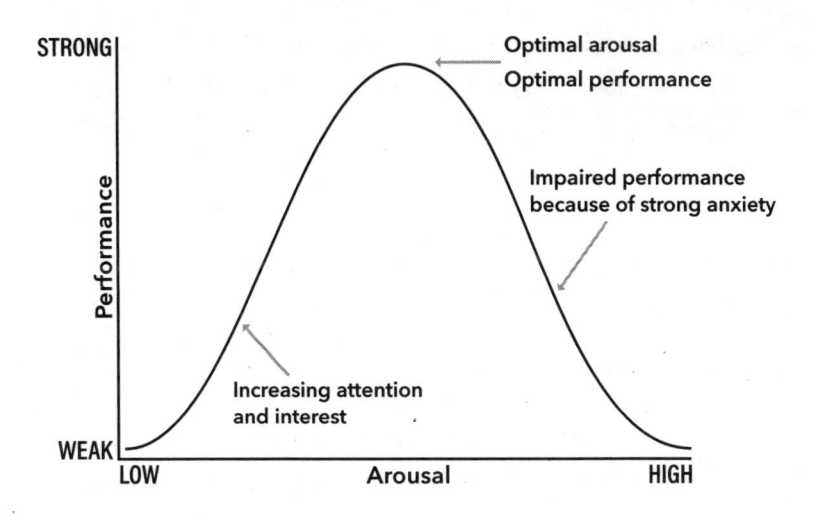

The left, which indicates low arousal, equates to someone saying, "I don't care," which means they wouldn't be motivated, so they won't perform at their best. With high arousal on the right, it's as if they're saying, "I can't handle this" (as described above), so they'll be overwhelmed and it will be hard to perform at their best. The sweet spot in the middle is when they tell themselves, "I care and want this to go well. And I can handle this," which allows them to feel the optimal amount of stress to perform at the highest level.

The question then becomes: What factors in our lives push us down one side or the other? According to Dr. Otis, it's our reaction—and not the event itself—that tips the scale.

As high achievers, we are going to have challenges and work stresses. Multiple deadlines and responsibilities are par for the course when you're a high-performing professional. And that won't overwhelm you as long as you perceive it as manageable. So our goal is to keep you at this sweet spot in the middle of the curve, where you have a moderate level of stress that will help you perform optimally.

The issues arise when you have additional stressors in your life that are piling up and make the load feel like too much to bear. We've already addressed some of the most significant *internal* sources of stress:

Unbalanced Thinking and Perfectionism (Essential #1)
Unhealthy Behavioral Habits and Lack of Self-Care (Essential #2)
Worry and Negative Self-Talk (Essential #3)

Now, in order to keep you from moving to the far right of the Yerkes-Dodson curve and feeling overwhelmed, we need to focus on the *external* stressor that comes up most with my high-achieving patients—and that, as we established above, is relationships. That means relationship issues with family, friends, coworkers, and romantic partners, as well as scrutiny by people on social media. And conversely, we have to explore how healthy relationships can act as buffers.

But how do these social stressors make our existing professional and personal challenges feel like too heavy a burden to carry or, in their healthiest incarnation, help us stay at the top of the curve? Say, for example, you have a major deadline coming up at work. Even though there's a lot riding on the outcome, you feel energized and able to zero in and get it done because you have people in your life encouraging you or helping you carry the load. But, if you're dealing with a difficult relationship at the same time—a breakup with your partner, pressure from your parents, unreasonable coworkers, an unkind boss, a frenemy who perpetually introduces doubt—the stress of trying to navigate both work and home life may feel like too much to handle.

Similarly, surrounding yourself with people who sap your energy or who sway you to do things that are out of character and feel negative— from gossiping to drinking too much—takes a toll. The same is true of being isolated. Loneliness, after all, isn't just being alone. It's the perception that no one is there for you or has your back. When that happens, you move from performing at your best (the top of the curve) to struggling to focus or even complete an assignment (the downside of the curve).

So it's crucial that you notice how being around certain people impacts you. Try to strategically maximize your time with those who uplift, encourage, support, and inspire you—that's what will help keep you in the sweet spot of the curve and being your best. Minimize your time with people who contribute to you feeling distressed, discouraged, or drained, or suck you into unhealthy behaviors or social comparison.

STRONG RELATIONSHIPS HELP US THRIVE

In his book *Cognitive Behavioral Therapy Made Simple*, Dr. Seth Gillihan observes that "nothing has a bigger impact on our well-being than our closest relationships...and we can tolerate just about anything if our relationships are strong and supportive."[3] Research underscores what Dr. Gillihan is saying: Healthy relationships increase feelings of well-being and decrease anxiety—and also help people *thrive*. Professors Brooke C. Feeney of Carnegie Mellon University and Nancy L. Collins of the University of California, Santa Barbara published a study in *Personality and Social Psychology Review* on social support and "thriving."[4] Dr. Feeney's takeaway? "Relationships enable us to not only cope with stress or adversity, but also to learn, grow, explore, achieve goals, cultivate new talents and find purpose and meaning in life."[5] Hear that? Hanging out with your close, caring friends can help you stay balanced and successful.

So if we know that relationships help us thrive, why do we as high achievers struggle to prioritize connection?

IN PURSUIT OF CONNECTION

When I'm sitting with a stressed-out patient in my office and I raise the importance of healthy relationships, they almost always intellectually understand. They nod and smile. Of course they do! They're brilliant! And they want to please me. But actually, creating and maintaining healthy connections on a consistent basis can be challenging.

Why? Well, high achievers perceive there to be multiple obstacles to sustaining strong relationships. The three hurdles I hear about most often are:

1. I have no time or energy!
2. It's easier to be by myself.
3. It's lonely at the top.

All of these hesitations are reasonable and are rooted in real issues. After all, relationships do take time, energy, and work. So in order to address these concerns and move forward to building these necessary connections, we need to do what we do best: take a hard look at where we're shining our flashlight and challenge our perceived hurdles.

I Have No Time or Energy!

I have rarely met an anxious high achiever who didn't frequently feel overextended. So it makes sense that, if you're constantly worried, overwhelmed, or burned out by your job and you have a jam-packed schedule, connecting with others can feel too effortful.

Instead of socializing, perhaps your go-to is to order food and spend what's left of the evening after work alone, binge-watching Netflix. And that's fine—sometimes. But not all the time. Not if you want to optimally manage stress and thrive.

Luckily, we have some tactics already in our arsenal to help us refuel our time and energy reserves and prioritize supportive relationships:

- **Recommit to self-care.** If your energy reserves are low, you need to break for... self-care! Say it together, people! When someone comes into my office talking about how they're too tired to see friends, it's a red flag to me that there's an issue with their self-care fundamentals. Ask yourself: Am I getting enough sleep? Am I eating well? Am I exercising a healthy amount? Make sure you're taking care of yourself, so you have the energy to spend time with others.
- **Keep things doable.** We're such pros at this! As you'll recall, the best way to create a habit and actually maintain it is to make it manageable. Plan something that doesn't take a ton of time or effort—but with a friend! Try a midweek coffee, a call during your walk home, or watching a movie together. Schedule in advance. And prioritize quality over quantity, choosing to reserve your weekly hangout for people with whom you feel genuine mutual appreciation.
- **"Can I let you know tomorrow?"** Don't be afraid to push PAUSE! If you've been asked to attend an event, do a favor, or fulfill a request that requires lots of time and energy, you can always say, "Let me look at my schedule. Can I let you know tomorrow?" Using this phrase, and giving yourself space to reflect and check in with yourself, can relieve the anxiety of having to respond immediately if you're not sure

if you want to agree. It will help you protect your time and energy. If anyone makes you feel like you have to answer instantly, that's a red flag. Ask yourself: Is this really an urgent issue? Or is this person not respecting my boundaries? Maybe they're anxious or stressed out—and pressing you. But just because someone else is stressed doesn't mean you need to feel compelled to be on their timeline. Especially in this world of constant communication, don't feel forced to make instantaneous decisions when you would be better served to pause.

DATING IS DATA COLLECTION

This issue of slowing down and even pausing often comes up with regard to dating. My high achievers are so anxious to find their person and check that off their list, sometimes they settle for whatever is most convenient. That's not a recipe for lasting love! I like to say: "Dating is data collection!" Rather than thinking, "I hope he likes me," remember that you're in the driver's seat. This is about your life, your energy, your stress levels. It's crucial to stay curious and collect ample data, giving yourself *time* before committing to anyone.

- Do you have compatible life goals, values, and lifestyle habits?
- Are they able to clearly and respectfully communicate their needs and show interest in learning about you and your needs, as well?
- How does your potential forever teammate respond when you tell them no or things don't go their way?

It's easy to appear charming and wonderful when everything is going well. A true test of someone's character is how they react when things don't go as planned. By taking your time to really learn who someone is, you can choose someone who adds value to your life—who encourages, supports, and inspires you to be the best version of yourself. Someone who accepts and appreciates you for who you are. You're awesome. You deserve to be loved and cherished.

It's Easier to Be by Myself

Here comes that perfectionism issue again, rearing its ugly (but very well-groomed) head. It pops up in places we might not expect. As we've discussed, high achievers often erroneously believe that they need to appear flawless in order to have value. They're afraid people won't accept them if they show vulnerability.

The problem is, when you're trying to appear perfect, you aren't being your authentic self. Because we, as humans, are innately quirky and imperfect. It's that realness that we connect to in each other; it's what helps us build relationships.

I often ask my clients, "Who is more relatable: Kendall Jenner in an airbrushed glossy magazine spread or Kendall Jenner caught on a bad hair day? We all know the answer. That's why we love Taylor Swift so much. It's not because she's so perfectly put together, though, of course, we appreciate her style. It's because she presents as living, breathing vulnerability. A raw nerve personified! She puts her foibles on parade and dares us to judge her. She tells us what feels like the truth. The fun of knowing people is uncovering their uniqueness—that's what solidifies bonds.

Missing out on this type of genuine connection is seriously problematic. Research shows that social support, the term psychologists use to describe encouragement you can access by being connected to other individuals, groups, or your community, is critical for both mental and physical health and, of course, enhanced resilience to stress.[6] In the TED Talk "What Makes a Good Life? Lessons from the Longest Study on Happiness," Robert Waldinger, director of the Harvard Study of Adult Development, explains, "The clearest message that we get from this 75-year study is this: Good relationships keep us happier and healthier. Period."[7]

The cost of missed connection is, therefore, substantial.

The other reason high achievers might find themselves avoiding social interaction is because they tend to gravitate toward their own kind—other ambitious folks. While there is arguably value in being in the company of intellectual equals or finding solidarity with colleagues in your field, you might find that these conversations also exacerbate your proclivity for comparison, amplifying feelings of inadequacy and anxiety. In social situations, especially with coworkers, my patients report worrying: "What if I'm not as good as I think I am? What if they just don't like me?" And then off they go, down the rabbit hole of distorted thinking—sometimes hitting the whole Troublesome Trifecta of cognitive distortions we know so well:

- **All-or-Nothing Thinking.** This distortion will have you believing that you need to be a fully capable rock star whom people gravitate toward, or you're a loser with nothing to contribute to a relationship.
- **Jumping to Conclusions.** Not only might you assume that others don't like you, but you also may think that, if they did, once they saw your vulnerabilities, they'd like you less.
- **Should Statements.** Causing additional self-doubt, this distortion makes you believe you *must* be able to appear perfect and be relatable at the same time. Everyone *ought to* like you. (There's that All-or-Nothing overlap again!)

Stop, Collaborate, and Listen

So what to do about social discomfort or insecurity? How do you avoid falling into these unhelpful thought patterns?

As we discussed when managing uncertainty, many high achievers feel unease around small talk in general. Cognitive distortions aside, it simply doesn't always come naturally. Honestly, I get it. Socializing can feel awkward, especially in situations where you don't know anyone—and you want to impress them. But it's also amazing how just talking to people can expand your world.

A few things to keep in mind:

- Remember, every friend you have started out as a stranger.
- You don't have to tell anyone your deepest, darkest secrets, but if you don't share anything personal (in other words, details about your life outside of work!), other people won't have a basis for connecting with you.
- No one is for everyone. Be who you are and your people will gravitate toward you.
- When you begin a conversation, bring your full attention to the other person. Listen and then respond based on what you learn. If, for example, they mention loving to travel, you might agree and say, "Me too! Where are you off to next?"
- Deep down, we're all still that awkward middle school kid and just appreciate someone who is kind and wants to talk to us. Be that someone.

Ultimately, letting people know you is essential because it leads to collaboration—the root of excellence and pulling up a seat at the table. Steve Jobs said it best: "Great things in business are never done by one individual; they're done by a team of people." He's right. Think about all sorts of things that could not have happened without cooperation and teamwork, each person contributing a particular expertise, life experience, or point of view.

Beyond that, collaborating with others can take some pressure off you to perform or produce. I know this can raise a slew of other issues: You might think working collaboratively will be seen as a sign of weakness or an indication that you can't succeed by yourself. You may be afraid to delegate because what if someone doesn't do the task as well as you could, or what if someone does it *better*? Maybe you feel like you don't know *how* to collaborate. That's okay! Trust yourself. The more you show up as a team member, the easier and more beneficial those interactions become. Think back on the times you had to learn a new skill: ride a bike, drive a car, start a new job. Now those all seem ordinary, innate, because you've done them so often. You just have to start.

> **Pro Tip:** Be the teammate of your own dreams. Someone who is thoughtful, kind, and competent, who makes room for a diversity of voices, ideas, and experiences. Someone who communicates clearly and respectfully, appreciates other people's strengths, and listens at least as much as they speak, if not more, to give everyone an opportunity to contribute.

ASK DR. A

Question: Is connecting through social media a good thing to do?

Dr. A: It depends. If you feel anxious, envious, or not good enough every time you scroll, listen to that. If you feel energized and delightfully entertained by Instagram, Facebook, or other platforms, or they help you grow your business, then some time on social may be okay. People do meet over social. Just always remember: Likes and followers are not the same as having friends. And managing the amount of time on an app is wise, particularly if you find yourself choosing your phone over in-person interactions. If you start

> feeling behind and struggling with social comparison, that's a signal to take a hiatus and work on balanced self-talk like, "I am enough exactly as I am." Because you are.

It's Lonely at the Top

In their determination to be the best and prove their worth, my high achievers have often spent years focusing solely on their jobs or academic endeavors, prioritizing their professional network over their social circle and intimate partnerships. As a result, it's not uncommon that my clients feel like they don't have anyone in their lives who understands or genuinely cares about them. No real friends they can count on in tough moments. Like my clients who don't know whom to list as their emergency contacts.

They're lonely.

Loneliness is the price many high achievers believe they need to pay in order to succeed. They often defend their choice to ascend alone. But in an ironic twist, isolation is often what *prevents* them from succeeding. In fact, in his 2023 "Letter from the Surgeon General," Dr. Vivek Murthy referred to loneliness as an "epidemic" and noted, "In recent years, about one-in-two adults in America reported experiencing loneliness." And that impacts our overall health profoundly. "The mortality impact of being socially disconnected is similar to that caused by smoking up to 15 cigarettes a day," Dr. Murthy wrote. The solution? You guessed it: healthy connections. He encouraged, "Each of us can start now, in our own lives, by strengthening our connections and relationships. Our individual relationships are an untapped resource... They can help us live healthier, more productive, and more fulfilled lives."[8]

And this impacts our careers, too. "A person's feeling of loneliness does relate to lower job performance,"[9] according to Hakan Ozcelik of California State University, Sacramento and Sigal G. Barsade of the University of Pennsylvania, the academic researchers behind a 2018 study, "No Employee an Island: Workplace Loneliness and Job Performance."[10]

In isolation, we have no one to bounce ideas off, help put things in perspective, or celebrate our wins. Through no fault of our own, we find ourselves without the logistical and emotional resources we need—and sometimes we don't know how to ask for help. And in a kind of vicious cycle, high achievers are often ashamed to admit that they're lonely, seeing it as a failure. But loneliness is never an indicator of your worth. It's just a signal that it's time to get out and connect more with others.

LIFTING LONELINESS

Fortunately, loneliness doesn't have to be permanent. We can begin to lift that sense of isolation in surprisingly simple ways using actionable strategies that are easily implemented, even into our busy daily lives.

Micro-Moments of Connection

When we're lonely, we don't always believe we can connect and may have a heightened fear of rejection, so it's usually best to begin with baby steps. You can ease your way in through what psychologist Barbara Fredrickson, PhD, calls "micro-moments" of "positivity resonance." These are instances of fondness that happen "anytime two or more people—even strangers—connect over a shared positive emotion, be it mild or strong."[11] This can be as simple as having a two-minute conversation with a coworker who shares your love of soccer or making eye contact and smiling as you walk past someone on the street. Maybe it's as basic as complimenting the cuteness of a stranger's puppy! In this post-COVID world, a lot of my clients no longer go into the office every day, but, in terms of manifesting these moments, making an in-person appearance even once a week can make a world of difference in terms of stemming the sense of isolation.

These instances of warmth can foster a stronger sense of belonging. At work, that ultimately can also help you establish alliances, which raises your stock for possible promotions and being brought on for more important projects. So consider greeting colleagues with a smile and a "Good morning!" A little kindness goes a long way. After all, who doesn't want to work with someone who's accomplished, focused, and excellent, *and* whose presence lifts others up, as well?

Encouraging Others Makes Us Feel Good

There's a phrase in Chinese—*Jiāyóu* 加油—that means "add oil." It's what you say to cheer someone on. I've loved this concept since the first time I heard it. Although it's hard to translate precisely into English, it's used as an expression of solidarity, a spirited show of encouragement and confidence in another's abilities—often accompanied by a fist pump. There's something quite beautiful about this image of adding fuel to someone's fire, especially in moments of adversity. My version of it? *You got this!*

While slogging through your last uphill marathon mile or during an exceptionally difficult day at work, what's better than someone rooting for you, commiserating, and reminding you you're not alone? Giving a heartfelt "You got this!" to a friend, a colleague, or even a passing acquaintance feels good, too. Truly, one of the quickest ways to decrease your anxiety is to focus on helping others through their trials, tests, and tough times in life, with encouraging words and actions. It will energize you both.

Give Help, Get Happy

Beyond encouragement, volunteering to help others in practical ways can also be beneficial to everyone involved. Dr. Larry Dossey describes a powerful phenomenon called the "helper's high," or "a feeling, following selfless service to others, of elation, exhilaration, and increased energy, then a period of calm and serenity... said to be similar to that following intense physical exercise."[12] Engaging in even the smallest acts of kindness can enhance your own mental and physical well-being: lower stress levels, increase self-esteem, heighten happiness and satisfaction, lower blood pressure, and even increase longevity.[13] Knowing you can make someone else feel better just by showing up reminds you that you're not alone.

There are many ways to help others, from small acts that I call Everyday Energizers to larger contributions. Once again, it's about quality over quantity. It's important to keep these actions doable and realistic. Everyday Energizers, for example, take only a minute to do but will provide you with a burst of feel-good energy. You could open the door for the person behind you, hold the elevator for someone rushing to get in, or just remember to say please or thank you in daily interactions. If you have more time to invest, you could tutor people at your local library, help at an animal shelter, assist someone who is moving with their packing or unloading, or participate in a charity walk or run. You might even meet like-minded people.

> **Pro Tip:** Play to your strengths. Put your talents, unique skills, and expertise to work to help others. Just make sure you're being mindful of your limited time and energy so you don't burn out![14]

TAKE ACTION

Text "Happy Birthday" to people you care about. It's easy to add friends' and family members' birthday info to your calendar and set alerts to send them messages on their special days.

Bonus Boost: Call them to sing "Happy Birthday" or send a video in which you serenade them for their special day! It's fun and instantly stress-relieving, and it will almost assuredly make you *both* smile! Think about how nice it feels when someone acknowledges you. Be the person who creates that good feeling for others.

WHO ARE YOUR EASY PEOPLE?

Of course, connecting with others isn't only about offering a helping hand. It's also about finding your people—the individuals who make you feel good and will support you on your path to being a happy high achiever no matter what. I call them your Easy People. These folks are accepting and kind. They allow you to be yourself and never make you prove or defend yourself. They're simply nice to be around. And they come in all shapes and sizes. There are the casual connections that add bright spots to every day: a colleague who sends you silly memes every morning; a barista at your coffee shop who shares your taste in music; the crossing guard who always gives you and your child big high fives as you walk to school. And then there are the lasting closer connections that deserve more of your time and attention: your brother who invites you over on weekends to chill on his couch to watch sports or mindless TV, your best friend from childhood or college who texts or calls weekly to keep up with your life and has you laughing within minutes. These are the kinds of relationships you want to encourage and cultivate. They help you relax and shift your focus from your internal, unhelpful cognitive distortions to the external, reality-based present moment—in which you are appreciated.

> **Pro Tip:** In this chaotic digital age, it's easy to get distracted. Remember to stay as present as possible when interacting with the important people in your life—so that they *feel* important and valued around you. As famed American writer Kurt

> Vonnegut asserted in his "autobiographical collage" *Palm Sunday*, "The secret to success in every human endeavor is total concentration."[15] In the personal realm, this means putting down your phone, making eye contact, and listening without thinking about what you're going to say next or about that email you need to send. We can feel it when someone is truly paying attention.

TAKE ACTION

Ready for your post-meetup check-in? You've just returned home from hanging out with a friend. How did this person impact your feelings, thoughts, and behaviors? How do you know whether you want to continue hanging out? Ask yourself the questions below. Be honest.

1. How do I feel physically? Do I feel more energized or relaxed, or do I feel drained, uncomfortable, or tense?
2. How do I feel emotionally? Do I feel motivated, joyful, or peaceful, or do I feel anxious, frustrated, or discouraged?
3. Do I feel seen, understood, and valued, or do I feel dismissed, judged, or criticized?
4. Did I engage in any unhelpful self-talk or actions when I was with this person?
5. How did I feel at the end of the meetup? Am I glad I went or relieved that it's over?
6. When I think about seeing this person again, how do I feel? Am I excited and happy to continue our connection? Or do I dread the possibility of another evening?

Your answers will offer valuable information!

WHO ARE YOUR UN-EASY PEOPLE?

You know who these folks are, don't you? The people in your life who tip you over the Yerkes-Dodson curve into overwhelming stress and anxiety. *No, thanks!*

After a hangout, these are the people who leave you thinking, "Wow, that was intense. I'm exhausted. Why did I agree to bail that person out—again?" It's so important to identify these thoughts when they arise. It's not about judging them as a person. It's using discernment about who you want to spend time with based on how they affect you. It's about being aware of how others impact your thoughts, feelings, behaviors, and energy so you can limit your interactions and avoid being catapulted into a negative headspace. This could be someone you're dating, a family member, or a friend who only talks about themselves, constantly manufactures crises, or often finds reasons to be angry at you. When you were with this person, did you find yourself complaining more or getting sucked into hateful trash talk about others? Making unhealthy and uncharacteristic choices like spending boatloads of money or drinking tons of alcohol? Did you find yourself defending your choices and having hurt feelings? If so, then minimize the time you spend with them.

The trouble is that some people are more difficult to distance ourselves from than others. For instance, my patient Robyn confided in me that she was struggling with her boyfriend. He constantly belittled her, making digs like, "You talk too much," or "What's wrong with you? Why are you so sensitive?" Then he'd give her the silent treatment to show his displeasure. In addition to his punitive behavior, she never knew which version of him she was going to get, and it negatively impacted her ability to focus fully on other things. She was constantly walking on eggshells. She finally decided she'd had enough and broke up with him. As hard as that was, Robyn told me she ultimately felt so much better with him out of her life. She found she could not only concentrate better at work but had more time to be with people she actually enjoyed!

> **Pro Tip:** To distinguish the Easy People from the Un-Easy ones, ask yourself: Is this someone who helps me think, feel, or act in healthy, balanced ways? Someone I truly have fun with, and I feel good about myself when I'm with them? Or is this someone who zaps my energy and creates stress, bringing out the worst in me?

THE EASY FRIDAY NIGHT RULE

Even the healthiest relationships involve disagreements, especially at the end of a long, stressful workweek. This is especially true for my high-achieving patients who tend to partner up with other high achievers who are also toiling extremely hard. Conflict frequently arises when they try to address some lingering logistical issue or thorn on a Friday evening, when they're exhausted and, for instance, hurrying to meet up with friends for dinner. To keep conversations constructive, try using my Easy Friday Night Rule.

Timing is everything. And Friday nights are not the moment to talk with your romantic partner, roommates, family members (or really anyone) about bills, difficult or potentially contentious topics, or what you wish they had done differently that week. Instead, allow yourself and the people around you time to decompress from the workweek, whether that means enjoying takeout, a favorite magazine, or a good rom-com. Easy Friday Nights are about practicing kind, healthy, and realistic expectations of others and yourself.

If there are thoughts, feelings, or issues that need to be addressed, plan a Saturday Check-In. Or strategically choose a different day. Ask yourself: When would *you* have the best, most patient reaction to something? Capitalize on that! Tired, hungry, and rushing are not optimal conditions for having a productive—or pleasant—conversation. So, schedule it for when you are rested, well fed, and have ample time to talk. You're likely to get a better response. Ideally, try to do this weekly. Agree on the day, so you're both on the same page and know what to expect.

BOUNDARIES ARE YOUR FRIENDS

It's not always easy to "break up" with people who negatively impact your thoughts, feelings, and behaviors. Nor do you always want to. Maybe they're family members or coworkers you can't easily avoid. When that's the case, it's important to know how to set clear boundaries. Letting people know what you are and aren't okay with is actually an opportunity to enhance the quality of your relationships. Take my patient Luke, who was having issues with a coworker who bombarded him with late-night texts, messages, and emails. To manage his stress levels as someone who worked from home, we knew it was important for him to create concrete distinctions between work hours and downtime. He didn't want to offend anyone or appear to be slacking, but he also recognized that he didn't optimize his time, energy, or sleep when he was thrust into a stress spiral by to-dos at ten o'clock every night. Instead, he reached out to his coworker and explained that any texts after 8:00 p.m. would be answered the next morning. Ultimately, this shift was a huge relief for him and allowed him to bring more fervor to work in the morning, when his problem-solving skills were more attuned.

YOU CAN SAY NO!

One of the elements that made Luke's situation challenging for him as an anxious high achiever was that it played against his impulse to people-please. According to psychotherapist Sharon Martin, MSW, LCSW, in her book *The CBT Workbook for Perfectionism*,

"People-pleasing is a compelling need to do things to make other people happy, have them like us, or to avoid conflict, even when doing so causes us problems."[16] You can see how this might be an issue. When you're compromising your own needs to placate others, the person losing out is you. This isn't the basis upon which you build strong, lasting relationships with Easy People. After all, it's unsustainable and inauthentic, which leads to resentment and burnout.

And why are high achievers so inclined toward people-pleasing? It goes back to that darn perfectionism again. High achievers say yes because they worry that otherwise people will think they're incompetent and can't handle what's being thrown their way. They want everyone, especially their higher-ups, to think there's nothing they can't do. "Because perfectionists doubt their worth and abilities," explains Martin, "they seek validation by trying to do the right thing, say the right thing, looking perfect, and meeting others' expectations."[17] So they say yes when asked if they can handle yet another assignment, though they're already drowning in current projects. When it comes to personal relationships, they'll agree to plans or responsibilities they don't want simply to be liked or loved. And it's at the detriment of their own happiness and achievement.

That's why learning to say no is an important and empowering lesson. As Steve Jobs said, "It is only by saying no that you can concentrate on the things that are really important." When you say no:

- **It protects your precious time and energy.** Being overcommitted and spread thin hampers your ability to be fully engaged in any one thing and have sustainable achievement.
- **It is a boundary-setter.** Saying no in a kind, respectful, and firm way is a true indication of what is manageable in that moment.
- **It leaves space for you to find your passion and purpose.** I love the phrase, "Saying no is really saying yes." The more

you say no, the more room you create to say yes to things that really advance you, excite you, or fire you up.

SAYING NO WITH KINDNESS

It can be fine, even good, to decline, as long as you do it with grace. Here's how:

- Don't promise anything you won't deliver. Don't add, "Let's make plans to hang out next week!" when you don't mean it.
- Tell the truth, even if it means avoiding details. You can say, "I'm sorry, but I already have plans," even if those plans are to sit on your couch. You don't need to provide justification for your no.
- Consider including phrases like, "Thank you for thinking of me," or "I'd love to, but I won't be able to make it that day," to let someone know that it's not personal.
- If you have to meet with someone who's challenging or sucks your time, timebox it, limiting the task to a finite period by saying, "I'm only available during this time."

ASSERT YOURSELF

Though it may seem daunting, it's definitely possible to be both kind and firm. In just about every relationship, assertive communication wins the day. That sweet spot between being passive and aggressive is respectful, direct, and clear. Passive communication tells others: *I respect you, but you don't have to respect me.* Aggressive communication declares: *You will respect me, but I don't respect you.* Assertiveness says: *I respect you and I expect and deserve the same from you.*

Assertiveness can help prevent you from complying with people's unfair requests out of fear or insecurity—and also discourage you from making unreasonable demands of others. Finding that balance can sometimes be a challenge, but it is especially important for high achievers, who are inclined to both passively people-please and expect perfection from everyone around them, appearing controlling or hypercritical.

> **Pro Tip:** Watch out for over apologizing! Many high achievers with people-pleasing tendencies struggle with repeatedly saying sorry. If they need to say no, voice a different opinion, or worry they inconvenienced someone, they feel compelled to keep apologizing. But saying sorry multiple times is unnecessary and can even feel off-putting to others. So, say a sincere sorry and then move forward. Or shift your apology to an appreciative statement. For example, in my emails, instead of apologizing for taking a little longer than usual to respond, I like to use the phrase, "Thank you so much for your patience." That way, you've acknowledged the other person's time without diminishing yourself.

Assertive communication is especially useful when you want to avoid putting someone on the defensive. Of course, it doesn't ensure a positive interaction every time, but it will make you more likely to be heard and respected. An added plus—it can help you feel less stressed at social events because you're now better equipped to navigate interpersonal situations, responding clearly and effectively to whatever comes your way.[18]

One way to approach speaking assertively, maneuvering through challenging interactions, is to use certain fundamental structures when speaking. For instance, "I feel _____ when _____ happens. I would really appreciate it if _____." When possible, avoid using the word "you" in the initial declarative statement, which can put people on edge and make them feel blamed. For example:

- When a coworker showed up later than promised and delayed a meeting: "I felt concerned and stressed when we weren't able to start the meeting on time. I would really appreciate it if you gave me a heads-up in advance next time if you're going to be running late."
- When your significant other isn't making time to focus on you: "I feel sad at the end of the day when we just turn on the TV and don't talk. It would mean so much to me if we could allot twenty minutes after dinner to hang out without distractions."

Years ago, to help the front office staff at our therapy practice assertively navigate challenging situations with clients, I came up with a system called B.L.I.P.S. As in, *Don't worry—it's just a blip* (a phrase that became a go-to in our office). Here's how it works: When you have to manage a difficult professional situation, you treat the exchange as simply a blip on your radar, a *moment* in your day. Don't let it be something you take home, stress about, or lose sleep over. Instead:

Breathe. Exhale! Sometimes we have a tendency to hold our breath when stressed, which only makes us more tense. Focus on practicing slow, deep breathing to relieve stress and tension in a difficult situation.

Listen. Most people just want to feel they are being heard and are more likely to remain calm when they see you are trying to hear and understand them.

Interact with kindness. Keep perspective in the moment to stay balanced—remember that this is one of many interactions you'll have during your workday and throughout your week. Maintaining your professional, kind composure is one of the most powerful tools you have in your control. It helps set the tone for the interaction and makes the situation much less likely to escalate and more likely to be resolved quickly and positively. Validate you've fully heard what the person said—what their request or concern is—before challenging it in any way.

Play as a team. Cultivate a sense of unity. In a professional situation, you may be working toward the same goal as the person with whom you are struggling, or at least you both likely want a resolution. Shine your flashlight on the way you're aligned rather than on your differences.

Self-care. After a hard conversation, you need to decompress. Take a few minutes to walk around the block, enjoy an Everyday Treat, or practice some other quick self-care.

So, stay assertive to cultivate healthy relationships, an invaluable step toward effectively managing your stress and becoming a happy high achiever. Next up? Slaying those *shoulds*.

You're doing great! You got this! *Jiāyóu!* (See how I did that?)

TOP TAKEAWAYS

- Excellence is a collaborative endeavor.
- Even micro-moments of connection can change your trajectory—and someone else's!
- Find your Easy People! Notice how others impact your energy and stress levels.
- *No* is a magic word that protects your energy and opens you up to more important yeses.
- Assert yourself! Difficult moments are just B.L.I.P.S.

ESSENTIAL #5

TRANSFORM *SHOULDS* TO CANS

Peace is the result of retraining your mind to process life as it is, rather than as you think it should be.

—Dr. Wayne W. Dyer

I should be doing more. I should be able to handle all of this. I should already be further ahead than I am. I should have known—how could I have been so stupid?

Oh, should-ing oneself: truly, the hallmark of a high achiever's anxiety. It's that pesky self-doubt and perfectionism popping up where they're not wanted again.

If any of these phrases, or related concerns, sound familiar to you, then I'm afraid you've fallen prey to the shoulds.

At first glance, these statements may seem harmless, almost like informal ways of pushing yourself or setting goals. But I'm sorry to say, they're quite detrimental, standing in the way of you meeting your lofty goals.

Why? Well, as we know from Part One, the Should Statement (also known as should-ing) is a menacing member of the Troublesome Trifecta. For our purposes here, a "should" is a self-criticism, a judgment, or, ultimately, an act of avoidance that resists the reality of a situation or person. It's about self-reproach instead of finding a fix. It suggests a desire to go back in time and correct a poor choice, for the world to work differently, for *people* to be different. It suggests that you must be lazy or not good enough unless you're following a specific metric set by others. It suggests that you're falling down on the job or aren't valuable if you decide not to do something, even if you're ambivalent.

I should have gone to sleep earlier. I should apply for a fancier job. They should have given me that promotion. I should be able to run a marathon. I should want *to run a marathon.*

In other words, shoulds are focused on the negative: how you *don't* want things to be or ways in which you—and others around you—*must* or *ought* to be better. And as we also know from our previous work together, this kind of unbalanced self-talk is not helpful. It keeps us stuck without offering constructive action steps for change. The shoulds are also a common pitfall for perfectionist high achievers, who tend to give themselves a relentlessly hard time.

But aren't you just setting high standards for yourself? Unfortunately, no. If anything, you're setting yourself up for defeat! In fact, "You're undermining your self-esteem and potentially increasing feelings of depression, anxiety, and shame," writes psychotherapist and author Sharon Martin, MSW, LCSW. "Ultimately, self-criticism makes us feel worse about ourselves, and it's hard to do better when we're yelling and calling ourselves derogatory names."[1]

Not to belabor the marathon metaphor, but if you were cheering someone on at the end of a race, would you encourage them by shouting, "You should be going faster! You should have already finished! You should have trained harder!"? No! Because that's counterproductive, it's unkind, and it doesn't help anyone thrive.

Should-ing is self-flagellating, not motivating. It makes us feel defeated, like we're never good enough. And like worrying, shoulds do not promote problem-solving. As we know, there's a vast difference between berating yourself for your behavior and, conversely, examining your behavior and strategically choosing a different path. The goal, therefore, is to accept reality as it is instead of dwelling in regret and frustration. That's not because we condone an unpleasant situation, but because we need to face the facts so we can be empowered to decide how to act. Instead of existing in a state of judgment or ambivalence, we succeed when we accept the truth of our circumstances and make actual, concrete decisions about how best to proceed. That's how we begin to create and meet realistic goals, propelling forward motion. We turn our *should*s into *can*s.

Early on in this book, we began the process of learning to poke holes in our shoulds. But the high achiever's habit of should-ing is so entrenched that we need to go deeper, unpacking and offering strategies for the particular ways it plays out in our daily lives. After all, challenging how we think things ought to be is a lot to ask when we've spent our entire lives thinking in terms of what we *should* be achieving.

The first step is to get good at identifying our shoulds so we recognize when this cognitive distortion is flaring up.

HOW YOU *SHOULD*

In my experience, there are three primary types of shoulds blocking the path to an excellent life:

- should-ing yourself
- should-ing others
- should-ing situations

We're going to learn how to catch and conquer all three. Away we go!

SHOULD-ING YOURSELF

How many times a day are you should-ing yourself? Telling yourself that you ought to have done things better? How do the shoulds make you feel?

As we established, shoulds keep you trapped by spotlighting what's "wrong" with you or how you're lacking. While it may seem like you're using them to keep yourself on course, you're actually just beating yourself up. I can't say this enough: Constant self-criticism causes anxiety, guilt, and feelings of inadequacy, which paradoxically make you less likely to do the very thing about which you are should-ing yourself. In other words, should-ing yourself often makes you feel too defeated to do what you think you should do.

As debilitating and paralyzing as a should spiral can be, thankfully, this cognitive distortion is straightforward to catch: You just stay alert for the word "should" in your thoughts and speech. Fascinatingly, the more you raise your awareness about shoulds, the more you'll notice their rampant frequency in society. Yep, shoulds are all around us, which is part of why we internalize them. You'll hear other people should-ing all over themselves, regularly. *I should go to the grocery store, the gym. I should call my mom. I should finish this brief. I should have a salad instead of this burger.* Just wait and see!

TAKE ACTION

At first, it can be easier to spot other people's shoulds than catch your own. For the rest of today or the next time you're with a group of people, keep a tally of how many shoulds you hear bandied about. You may be surprised by the number! This will help tune you in to your own unhelpful slips and prime you to keep your ears open.

Understanding the Real Why

Whether it turns out you should yourself ten or one hundred times a day, good for you—you've caught those distortions! Begin by giving yourself credit for that. Your journey has begun! Being aware of your shoulds affords you the opportunity to take action to overcome them.

Next up, let's gain clarity on the root of these unhelpful distortions, an important step toward reclaiming control, getting unstuck, and directing your energy with intention.

Because while they're less than ideal, shoulds are also signals to investigate further. They're signs that something is unbalanced in your thoughts that's triggering self-reproof and insecurity. They stand in for or mask other unmet needs and anxieties. One way we get to the bottom of this is to pause when we stumble upon a should and ask ourselves questions to get to the bottom of the issue. Ask yourself: I wonder why I'm telling myself I should do this? Why is this a "should"? What is it really about?

More specifically, there are three questions I suggest you ask yourself to get clear on what's fueling a particular should:

1. **Is this should something I think would be "helpful"?** For example, *I should eat less sugar. I should turn off my phone an hour before bed every night. I should switch from drinking soda to drinking water.*
2. **Is this something "I want" for myself?** For example, *I should start writing in the nice journal I bought for myself last week. I should plan a lunch date once a month with a friend so I can give myself a pleasant activity.*
3. **Is this something I'm telling myself "I must" do or be?** (Note: This one may also sound like "I'm supposed to" or "I ought to.") For example, *I should be able to do this without help. I should be able to make this unhealthy marriage work. I should be a size 4.*

The first two should categories are fundamentally about trying to *help* yourself or give yourself something you *want*. They are at least rooted in honoring your actual desires, though the goals are framed in a way that feels overwhelming. You may feel unmotivated in the face of a too-challenging objective, but these are, at core, about trying to meet your own vision for success and happiness.

The third, conversely, isn't even about what you want. This stand-in for "I must" or "I'm supposed to" is about kowtowing to the expectations of other people or our society. These are things you think you're supposed to do in order to look cool or smart or beautiful or worthy, but not because you actually enjoy or value the act itself. This "must" category is particularly prevalent among high achievers because it gets jet-fueled by their pressure-cooker, perfectionistic thinking—an all-or-nothing belief that there is only one "right way" to be, act, or live. That, in turn, gets compounded by the distorted thought that, if you don't adhere to these specific expectations, you'll somehow be wrong, defective, incompetent, or a disappointment. It's a cognitive distortion, wrapped in a cognitive distortion, wrapped in a cognitive distortion (aren't brains great?).

Taking Down the Helps, Wants, and Musts

Fortunately, once you know which of the three thoughts is underlying your should, you're ready to broach the issue with strategic intention. Ask yourself: How do I want to address this? What action do I want to take? In this circumstance, are you inclined to acquiesce to your must, for example by making a decision based on what you imagine others might think is best, or do you want to make a decision based on what you actually want for yourself? Once you realize you're feeling bad about not yet applying for that fancy job primarily because you feel you ought to, do you still choose to throw your hat in the ring? Maybe. Maybe not. Either way, at least you're mindfully deciding for yourself, which is where your power lies.

What does this look like in action? Let's take them one at a time.

It Would Help

Let's start with the classic, "I should be going to the gym more." This is something I hear from my high-achieving clients daily. Sometimes it's because they want to exercise but have trouble making time. Sometimes it's because they feel they must work out for hours every single day or it doesn't count. My patient Josie's long hours at work had her neglecting her health. She thought she *should* go to the gym. So I asked, "Do you think it would be helpful for you to go, do you want to go, or are you telling yourself you must go?"

"Honestly," Josie said, crinkling her brow, "I don't want to go to the gym. It's not a *must*. I just think it would be helpful if I went."

This made sense. After all, Josie wanted to improve her fitness and better manage her stress. She knew the combination of a sense of accomplishment and endorphins left her feeling good afterward.

So we switched up her self-talk. She practiced out loud: "It would be *helpful* for me to go to the gym." The simple act of replacing the word "should" with the relevant new word can give you new agency and insight, adjusting how you feel about a given should over time. Once Josie recognized her purpose, she could move forward by creating a doable starting goal so that she didn't have to walk around feeling like she'd failed at going *every day*. By integrating exercise in a realistic way, she turned her "should" into a manageable "can," which is what creates momentum and motivates us to maintain a habit.

I Want To

We all have ways we legitimately want to improve or enjoy our lives but find challenging to adopt. This comes up regularly for high achievers because we tend to prioritize work instead of breaks. The solution, in this case, is quite similar to the "It would be helpful" variation: shifting self-talk.

Say, for example, you joined a meditation group. You love the people and how well the practice promotes peace and calm, but at the end of a long workday, you don't always feel like attending. Instead of thinking, "I should go," what if you said, "I want to go"? Simply by shifting your language to reflect a driving desire rather than scolding yourself about what you "should" do, you give yourself a different level of ownership over the choice. You allow yourself to acknowledge that, though you feel tired and pressed for time, you committed to this activity because it makes you feel good, during and afterward. That's a positive, bolstering reason to make the effort once a week.

Something I Must Do

"I must" is a slightly different beast in that it's externally motivated and about insecurities versus your true inclinations. My anxious financial analyst patient Ben came to me with a related conundrum: "I feel like I should apply for the new impressive job my friend Jack told me about."

But Ben didn't think it would be helpful, as it involved a longer commute and less pay, and he didn't want the job. He was happy where he was! He just felt like he ought to apply because of how it appeared to others. This job was something he was *supposed* to want. He looked at me, eyes wide. "Is this a 'must'?"

Realizing a should is motivated by a must gives you power because it creates enough distance between you and the potential action to gain perspective. Rather than feeling stuck in guilt or shame, you can ask yourself: Is this even something I want? and make an informed decision. It was time for Ben to call up some of those assertive communication skills we learned and set kind but firm boundaries with Jack.

Ben realized that he was worried about appearing complacent, and his resulting anxiety was worsening by the day. So we helped him generate some new and improved self-talk. And that's where the "cans" come in again...

Getting to "I Can"

"I can" is a statement that increases your motivation to take action. That's right! It's the diametric opposite of a disempowering should. Instead of suggesting that you aren't up to the task or don't have the energy, it affirms your power. When you implement it, you're literally saying, "I am capable of doing this. I am able." It transforms your awareness into action. That's impactful! Even a step beyond *wanting* to do something, "I can" is a declaration of your competence. And though the notion of believing in yourself might seem corny, the effect of that is very real. Believing you will be able to achieve your goal is crucial in order to be motivated to do it. Saying "I can" is acknowledging your agency within the reality of your situation. It facilitates effective goal setting based on what is actually possible. When you get to a genuine "I can," that leads to an achievable goal.

When trying to get to the bottom of your "I can"—or doable goal—it's normal to hit snags. Even a statement like "I'll try" or "I guess" implies hesitation. Keep refining and negotiating until you're beyond that. When you can say "yes!" without hesitation, you've found your can. For Josie, for example, that meant three thirty-minute workouts this week. The following week, twenty-minute workouts felt more realistic. The goalpost can shift weekly based on logistics, as long as the objective remains truly doable.

> **Pro Tip:** Give yourself a choice about the length, style, and setting for your workout instead of whether you exercise at all. You may wind up going longer than anticipated, and it helps you overcome the hardest part—starting.

"I can" looks like blocking off your calendar starting at 5:00 p.m. so you don't have to rush to meditation group at 6:30 p.m., and bringing a snack so you aren't tempted to head to dinner instead. It means staying in the job you like and telling a friend or colleague, "Thank you for the suggestion," just as my patient Ben did with his friend Jack.

By creating specific, manageable goals based on what you truly envision for yourself, you'll embody excellence in action.

TAKE ACTION

Next time you notice that you're should-ing yourself, try transforming that cognitive distortion into a can!

1. What is your should? Give yourself credit for catching it!
2. Ask yourself: What is my should really about?

    - Is it something **I think would be helpful** for me?
    - Is it something **I want** for myself?
    - Am I telling myself **"I must"** do this or be this certain way because of erroneous thinking?

3. Modify your self-talk by replacing "should" with the relevant more balanced, useful words:

    - "It would be helpful to ____ because ____."
    - "I want to ____ because ____."
    - Poke holes in the unbalanced "must"! "I feel pressure because ____."

4. Create an "I can" statement to identify a doable short-term goal and get unstuck! You *can* do it!

Gut Check Your Goals

While shoulds are inherently problematic, they're also amazing indicators about your deepest desires or interests—and dissatisfactions.

They're like neon signs telling you what you want to work on, your true goals. Say you find yourself thinking, "I should really stick to a budget." That's likely a signal that it would be helpful for you to improve your saving and spending habits. Maybe you're just having trouble mustering the energy to make changes, or it all feels too daunting and you don't know where to start. This is where you can use your should as a cue to create an actionable objective. After all, the key to sustainable success is identifying and meeting your goals.

Setting and achieving our aims is what moves us forward in our careers and also makes us feel good, bringing a sense of progress and satisfaction. But as we've already established, if those goals are based on unrealistic expectations, they have the opposite effect.

You've likely heard about how to create S.M.A.R.T. (Specific, Measurable, Attainable, Relevant, Time Bound) goals,[2] which can be a great way to systematically think about and write effective objectives. In practice, I've found my high-achieving patients don't always want to take the time to go through each of the five S.M.A.R.T. steps. And honestly, some have heard so much about S.M.A.R.T. goal setting that they balk at the mere mention of the acronym. So, for a streamlined approach, I ask the three questions below to help patients successfully set and complete goals. We want you to succeed! Before you commit time and energy to working toward an outcome, check in with these:

1. Is this something you *want* to work on?

This is always the first question I ask. And it's pretty eye-opening. After all, what's the likelihood of being productive when you're working toward a goal you don't actually care about meeting?

So when you set a goal for yourself, make sure it's something you *actually* want to work on. You need to choose WHAT you want for yourself. And know WHY you want it. Why is your target personally meaningful to you? Whether the objective is moving abroad, making more money, or meeting a romantic partner, ultimately the benefits need to outweigh the costs in your mind so you'll put in the work.

If your goal is important enough to *you* (not just what your parents, society, and others dictate you *should* want)—you won't quit. You may have to adjust your strategies more than once to accomplish your aim as circumstances evolve, but you'll be motivated to keep finding ways to move forward. So, decide what you want for yourself. Which brings us to your *HOW*...

2. Is your goal strategic?

Once you've determined that your goal is something you definitely want to work on, the question becomes: How do you create goals that can be explicitly achieved, checked off the to-do list that brings you so much joy? First, give your objective a concrete metric. For example, if you want to read more, don't simply vow to buy more books. Decide how many days a week you're going to read and for how many minutes. Have a way to monitor your behaviors. Use whatever is most convenient for you (checkmarks on a calendar, for instance, or smiley faces or notes in your planner). Create some specific, external system to track completion. That way you'll know when you're meeting (or even surpassing!) your goal and can derive satisfaction from the progress, creating momentum.

And make those metrics realistic! If you currently barely read at all, don't set yourself up for failure by pledging to read five days a week for two hours a day. Be honest with yourself about your starting point. Start small. I know it's hard. You want to make a big splash. You're a high achiever and your impulse is to go big. But let's begin by dipping a toe in. My favorite compromise: "at least" goals. "At least" is a secret weapon! It means that you establish a practical baseline while leaving yourself room to expand. For example, if you pledge to do *at least* one relaxing activity a week, you can always add more, but as long as you do *at least* one, you'll feel you've completed your goal. And that keeps your morale high!

Sometimes a goal is outside the realm of my patient's control. For instance, say you decide: "I want to get promoted in the next three months." If that's not aligned with your company's timeline, it simply won't happen no matter what you do. Instead, choose goals you can *directly* achieve—such as, "I can arrive to work on time to show my boss my commitment." Or "I can contribute at least one thoughtful comment at each morning meeting and come with resolutions ready." Put your best foot forward.

3. Is your goal doable?

Time for the ultimate gut check: We touched on the idea of doable goals previously, around making time for self-care and challenging perfectionism, so you're familiar with this concept. If your goal isn't based on realistic standards, then you're setting yourself up for failure instead of success. You caught all those shoulds—now's your time to transform them to cans!

So how do you know you've created a doable goal? Ask yourself: Do I believe I can accomplish this? If you don't believe it, then you need to make it smaller. Yep. Dead serious. Back to the drawing board! Because what's going to give you confidence and momentum is being able to achieve something, even if it's tiny. That's what keeps you from giving up. I always say, "Dream big, do the work, expect miracles." But you *have* to do the work. Otherwise it's just a wish. So if you catch yourself setting a goal that you don't believe you can meet, don't set it. Because that will impact your trust in yourself, too. Accept reality and take smaller strides, for now. Remember: A string of single steps completed is better than a large leap never taken.

I'm an ideal example: I love chocolate. I know it wouldn't be healthy to eat it in large quantities every day, but I would go bananas if

I couldn't ever have it. So instead of thinking I *should* avoid chocolate, I realize I *can* eat chocolate. But I can eat a few squares of delicious 70 percent dark chocolate each day and enjoy its mood-boosting benefits[3] instead of eating hot fudge sundaes. See? Doable goals don't feel like punishment or deprivation.

How will you ultimately know if your goals are doable? If you're doing them! If your monitoring shows you didn't complete your specific goals for the week, big or small, it's problem-solving time. Ask yourself: What made it hard to complete my goals this week? Am I setting objectives I don't really want to work on? Or were the aims just not doable enough? What could I do differently to make my goals more doable? How can I proactively overcome any issues that may hinder me?

Bottom line: Don't keep doing what isn't working. Modify as necessary to keep making progress. Keep setting doable goals. Keep troubleshooting. Keep moving forward.

SHOULD-ING OTHERS

Just when you thought we'd covered it, the should-ing continues—only this time, we're looking at should-ing others. Oh, you know what I mean: When you're a high achiever, those perfection-seeking standards sometimes accidentally get applied to the people around you. And yes, I'm sorry to say, that's a problem. "When we expect perfection from others and are intolerant of mistakes, we can damage our relationships," explains psychotherapist and author Sharon Martin, MSW, LCSW. "Nagging, criticizing, and focusing on what our loved ones are doing wrong erodes connection and open communication."[4] This is troubling in terms of bolstering your interpersonal relationships, which, as we learned, are so important to your continued happiness and success. But it's also an issue when it comes to professional relationships, key to making progress in your career.

I hear it from my patients on a regular basis. They come in feeling frustrated, often for legitimate reasons, grumbling phrases like: "He should be helping more. She should've known better. They should be more appreciative. He shouldn't be this difficult to talk to. They should be on time!"

Yep. We've all done it. Just like should-ing yourself, should-ing others is about judgment. When you should someone else, you shine your flashlight on what that person isn't doing well enough or what you wish were different about them. Unfortunately, should-ing others doesn't generally make you feel happy. So the person you're coming down on, either in your mind or directly, isn't the only one who suffers. When you should others even in your mind, you'll likely feel exponentially frustrated, resentful, or even anxious—especially if you're avoiding confronting the issue directly or are uncertain about how to move forward.

We know that feelings impact behaviors. So will feeling stressed or frustrated with someone help you interact well with them? Or find resolution? Not so much. Again, shoulds = stuck.

Action or Acceptance

As renowned psychologist Dr. Carl Rogers wrote in his book *A Way of Being*, "People are just as wonderful as sunsets if I can let them be...When I look at a sunset...I don't find myself saying, 'Soften the orange a little on the right hand corner, and put a bit more purple along the base'...I don't *try* to control a sunset. I watch it with awe as it unfolds."[5]

I know, I know. Easier said than done. It's not a simple task, looking at Fred in accounting and learning to appreciate his "work style." After all, you're probably thinking, "Fred really should soften the orange, if by that you mean ramp up his work ethic."

The thing is this: Even though it's common for high achievers to feel that they know the best way to get things done, people come in many stripes. And we have to learn to tolerate a different, albeit sometimes less urgent or efficient, approach to life. As long as people aren't hurting you or someone else, you need to let them do their thing as much as possible. That's partially because people don't like to be criticized or undermined, but also because you're unlikely to effectively change them anyway.

So what do you do when you notice you are should-ing others, in your thoughts or your words? As always, first give yourself credit for catching your should. Next, stay curious! Just like your *I should* self-talk was trying to tell you something, your *You should* is also a signal—to choose either action or acceptance!

Action

In this context, what is "action"? Well, action is *doing* what you actually need to do to remedy a fraught or untenable situation. Just as people should themselves instead of problem-solving, they often should others when what's really necessary is taking action—to address injustices or safety issues and/or to ensure that they and their needs are being respected. So your should may be an indication that it's time to set boundaries. (In cases of abuse or imminent threat, call 911 or enlist the help of a trained professional. It's beyond the scope of this book to truly discuss these topics; just please know you are not alone. And remember: You are a person worthy of respect and love.)

For everyday, non-crisis situations: Bring on the assertive communication!

Say you're working on an important group project with a hard deadline, and one colleague or classmate has not contributed his section by the mutually agreed-upon time. You may think, "He should've sent his part to us already! I finished mine last week. The project is due in just a few days!" You could waste time and energy sitting in that irritation. You could also confront this person, should-ing him to his face—which is just not useful. Think about how you feel when someone says *you* should do something. As humans, we typically recoil from being told what to do. Not effective! Instead, first confirm that there's no extenuating reason for his tardiness. Then, take action by saying something kind, but direct and firm, replacing "should" with terms like "helpful" and "I would appreciate." You could approach with something like: "I'm concerned because our project is due in a few days. It would be helpful if we could check in by phone or in person to discuss and ensure we meet our deadline. Are you available anytime today or tomorrow?"

Again, these proactive clauses give the listener a sense of what to do rather than focusing on what they did "wrong." Consider what you would respond better to:

"You should have caught that typo! This went out to the whole company and now we look like amateurs!"

Or:

"Going forward, I would appreciate if you could read documents over twice before sending so we ensure we catch any errors before it goes out to the entire staff."

You're a high achiever! You likely would have already harangued yourself for not catching the errant typo. You don't need someone else's should coming at you.

But does every desire or passing thought about should-ing others mean you need to take action? Nope. Again, life is about balance. There will be times when your urge to should another person can remain in your head. In that case, practice…

Acceptance

Okay, fine. But how do you know if a should is signaling a need for acceptance instead of action?

If this is not a situation where your needs are being disregarded, ask yourself: Why am I should-ing this person? Am I should-ing someone because they are not doing what I prefer them to do or think is the best decision? Is there an actual conflict or am I just irritated because they're not acting as I would?

If you tend to should others about everyday topics, which may mostly be about a difference in strategy or personality and not really a problem per se, it may be more useful to practice acceptance instead.

Acceptance means reminding yourself that people are people. Sunsets of varied shades. It means tolerating those variations. Others will make choices you wish were different and take actions that are less than ideal in your mind.

As a high achiever, I'll be honest: It's not always easy. You may be more frequently let down by others because of your tendency toward perfectionist standards. But if the other person's behavior is not causing a concrete problem in your life and is, rather, just rubbing you the wrong way, then it's not appropriate to bring it to their attention. After all, they're entitled to be different from you, even if, in this scenario, "different" feels synonymous with "worse."

It's also crucial to recognize that it is not your responsibility to "fix" other people. Many of my well-intentioned patients "just want to help" and report feeling almost obligated to tell others what they should do. This is especially the case with those who are in leadership roles at work and are used to wielding control. Remember: An unsolicited should is not your duty or even appreciated most of the time!

Instead, keep in mind that we're all just human. Ask yourself: Am I focusing on what I don't like about the person? Am I being overly critical or controlling? Am I accepting their freedom to make different choices?

Flip Your Focus

Once you catch and begin to conquer your own self-criticism, it's easier to look at others with kindness. Additionally, there are strategies that can help you see the object of your irritation in a more flattering light. Here are my top tools for no longer should-ing others and instead finding acceptance:

1. Focus on the fact that it's not intentional. When you realize that a person is not *trying* to frustrate, wrong, or stress you, how does it make you feel? Better! Recognizing that something is unintentional tends to take the wind right out of your angry sails. Most of the time, people are not intentionally making life difficult for you. They're just being themselves. That eccentric coworker of yours? She's not trying to annoy you with that New Age ringtone—that's just her jam.

2. Focus on positive aspects of the person. Instead of focusing on what you wish were different, acknowledge what the person does well. For example, instead of training your flashlight on the thought, "He should've done the dishes," try shifting to, "He didn't do the dishes, but he did take out the trash without me asking, he really listened rather than give unsolicited advice when I talked about my day, and he gave me a hug today during a tough moment." You don't necessarily need three positives to drown out that one negative, but the more the better!

The aim here is to help you keep perspective. If household chores are a chronic issue, you can choose action and assertively address that. But if they're not, or if your partner's idea of organizing is just dissimilar from yours, refocus your flashlight to highlight how that person is good, with the goal of balancing your thoughts. Then see how you feel.

What's the rule of thumb? Thoughts impact feelings, and feelings impact behaviors. If you keep focusing on someone's positive qualities and you start feeling better (less resentful, anxious, or frustrated), guess how your interactions with that person will probably go? Yes! Better! Again! And that may actually make it more likely that your partner will remember to do the dishes in the future.

3. Focus on the opportunity. When you identify a quality in a person that you think "should" be better, remember that's just your opinion. Instead of harping on what you don't like, look for how you may actually benefit from engaging with them. Find ways to use interactions with others to grow or enhance your skill set. Yep. That's right. Transform that initial annoyance into an instrumental opportunity.

A real-life example of this presented itself recently when I overheard a friend on the phone with his employee. The employee was expressing her frustration about one of their customers (a larger company that was making unique requests) and lamented, "They shouldn't be this difficult!" My friend acknowledged he understood how she felt and then noted: "This is definitely challenging, but it can also be useful to us because we wouldn't have thought of how to respond to these types of requests unless this company had raised the issue. Now we can develop standard operating procedures to use when similar situations arise." That's flipping your focus in action. That's *acceptance*.

TAKE ACTION

When was the last time you should-ed someone in your mind, when they weren't technically doing anything wrong? Practice bringing acceptance to the scenario by flipping your focus with these fill-in-the-blanks:

1. This may not have been intentional because:
2. This person may bother me in certain ways, but their positive attributes are:
3. This person could potentially bring an opportunity to learn new skills or meet new people because:

See if you can shift your perspective in order to feel less frustrated and move forward!

SHOULD-ING SITUATIONS

So here's the situation: Your boss gave someone else "your" promotion. Your presentation rocked, but the competing company got the gig. The person you're crushing on likes someone else. You find yourself thinking things like: "This shouldn't be happening! That should've gone differently. This should be easier. It should never have happened." Like should-ing yourself and should-ing others, should-ing situations—evaluating a circumstance or event with judgment—keeps you stuck and raises your anxiety. And when are you most likely to should your situation? In the swamp.

Into the Swamps

"We all have our turn in the swamp." That's what I tell my patients at some point during their treatment, their eyebrows furrowing. The swamps of life are times of great challenge, difficulty, or uncertainty. When you're dealing with things you never thought would happen to you. When you are facing harrowing trials you don't know how to navigate and have no idea what might happen or come next. In fact, often, what initially leads people to my doorstep is falling into the middle of a murky, nasty swamp. Especially for high achievers, who pride themselves on being able to handle almost anything, should-ing situations often transitions into self-judgment for reacting to and having feelings about the given difficulties.

Going through a divorce, losing your job, coping with the death of a loved one, getting injured in an accident, discovering your partner had an affair, dealing with the devastation of miscarriage, entering a new stage of life, aging, moving to a new city, finding yourself underemployed and financially struggling, coping with an unprecedented global pandemic...yep, welcome to the swamp.

The path to success is rarely as predictable or smooth as you've imagined, and high achievers' personal swamps often start where the "conveyor belt" ends. You know the one: the conveyor belt that started seemingly at infancy, that propelled you forward from straight As to athletic awards to college and graduate school acceptance to a competitive job—and don't forget securing a romantic partner along the way!—before jolting to a halt sometime in your twenties or thirties. It's my term for the deeply held belief, often repeatedly reinforced during childhood, that if you keep doing "the right thing," you will move predictably from one successful milestone to the next. But the reality is, at some point in life, you will inevitably get dropped off the conveyor belt...and into the swamp.

These moments often originate from events that are unexpected, imposed, and/or aversive. It is when plodding through this unforeseen muck that patients will often say: "This shouldn't be happening, Dr. A." For me—that's go time.

Because I absolutely understand. I don't want this to be happening to you, either. And do I know why it's happening? (I get asked this question a lot.) Humbly, I have no idea. What I do know is, if you keep telling yourself it "shouldn't" be happening, though it clearly is—if negating reality becomes the constant narrative—you'll stay stuck in your distress. You'll find yourself anxious, overwhelmed, frustrated, angry, sad, and/or scared. Because, as we know, shoulds drain our energy and can make us feel frustrated and resentful. They're a form of avoidance. Sometimes, in the swamp, you don't want to face reality. You just want to feel angry or frustrated about it. Which is reasonable. But when you focus on should-ing the situation—naming all the ways that you think it ought to be but isn't, rather than accepting what is and taking action—you'll feel as if your agency has been diminished. In other words, it will be harder to climb out of the muck.

So, I created a three-step "compass" to shift your thinking away from being bogged down and disempowered and toward successful traversing. Follow me!

Out of the Swamps

The process I developed for skillfully navigating a swamp, finding footing, and effectively coping with significant change is called EAO, which stands for "Empathy, Acceptance, Optimize." This is your "I can," a way to turn should-ing situations into personal and professional growth. And it's yours to use! As Darwin is sometimes attributed as saying, "It is not the strongest of the species that survives, nor the most intelligent that survives. It is the one that is most adaptable to change." So, the goal of EAO is to assist you as you adapt to the shifts in your life—in your career, home life, health, finances, relationships, or just day-to-day routine—and show you how to survive in your new reality. Finding a way forward and learning to adjust as necessary, to mitigate situational shoulds and find a new perspective like an open door, is essential for optimal long-term energy management and high achievement. After all, what is achievement if not continually moving onward and upward, toward each next challenge?

Step 1: Empathy. What would you say to a close friend who was going through a truly tough time? Would you mock, minimize, or judge their feelings? Or tell them, "Oh, just get over it. You'll be fine. Other people deal with so much worse!" Nope. You wouldn't. Why not? Because you know that's not nice—or helpful. And the last thing people need when going through a difficult time is judgment. You would be there for that friend. You would practice empathy—try to understand what they're going through and how they're feeling. You would listen. You would stay patient, curious, and respectful. You wouldn't immediately jump into telling them how they "should" feel or ways to "fix" things.[6] Remember: You deserve the same.

So, just like you would for a close friend, give yourself time to process when life gets hard. Notice how you are feeling. Because if you refuse to feel your feelings, they'll persist. Talk to a trusted confidante or counselor. It's okay and even helpful to say out loud: "I feel angry, frustrated, scared, overwhelmed, and/or disappointed." You don't need to do anything about the feelings. Just let yourself feel them. I promise, they won't last forever.

The one thing I can guarantee is that feelings change. Thank goodness for impermanence! No one emotion can be sustained forever. Your experience of feelings, their combination and intensity, varies over time. Meanwhile, instead of being self-critical, respond to yourself and your situation with patient curiosity and understanding to expedite the process of feeling better.

Step 2: Acceptance. As we've discussed, acceptance is the ultimate alternative to should-ing. It involves recognizing the facts of the situation as they actually are, not as you want them to be. Because this is going to put you in the strongest position when approaching a situation in order to overcome it.

So even—or *especially*—if your current situation seems wildly unfair or difficult, it's imperative that you face the facts. Denial, avoidance, minimizing, or raging against your circumstances—no matter how unfortunate—will not help you. It will make you feel worse. Kind of like running into a brick wall. To be absolutely clear, I don't mean that you have to agree with, condone, or even like your reality in any way. It's about acknowledging the truth so you can then channel your energy toward improving things—just as we discussed regarding setting goals. If you acknowledge what's happening, you give yourself the gift of agency to make decisions and move forward. It would be far-fetched, for example, to expect that anyone could like getting suddenly demoted. That's absurd. But unless you accept the fact that your job situation has changed, you will be unable to take the proper steps to find something new, to take the energy you've been using to resist and put it into navigating next steps. So in your given situation, ask yourself: What is motivating this should? What are the realities of my circumstances right now? What is making me feel frustrated, anxious, and stuck?

Step 3: Optimize. Optimizing is how we make your situation less effortful and more livable. It's learning to swerve when life throws you a curve. Specifically, it's about determining what you currently do and don't have control over—and then using what you *can* control to your advantage.

So how can you optimize when you find yourself in a swamp? Focus your attention, resources, and energies toward the things you still *do* have choice over. One great way to recenter is to return to your self-care fundamentals. You can usually choose, to some extent, what time you get up, exercise, eat, go to bed, and so on. You can plan pleasant activities to look forward to and build in Everyday Treats to bolster you. Make healthy choices and take control where you can.

One of my heroes, the Austrian psychiatrist and Holocaust survivor Viktor Frankl, wrote in his inspirational book *Man's Search for Meaning* that "everything can be taken from a man but one thing: the last of the human freedoms—to choose one's attitude in any given set of circumstances, to choose one's own way."[7]

You can't necessarily change the reality of your situation, but you can try to support yourself through it in the best possible ways. That is the ultimate "can." Truly, no matter what you are going through, you can choose to work on your self-talk. You can shift your shoulds, just as we did when you were should-ing yourself and others. Every thought you focus on will either help you adapt to the changes in your life and move you forward or will keep you overwhelmed and paralyzed. How you choose to think about your circumstances will profoundly impact how you experience them. The choice is always yours.

So whether you're should-ing yourself, others, or a situation, the key to getting unstuck is determining what's behind the should by taking an honest look, shifting self-talk, and trying to flip your focus to either a different perspective or the best way to take care of yourself. And with that clarity, we *can* move on to the next Essential!

TOP TAKEAWAYS

- Shoulds keep us stuck. Awareness, acceptance, and action move us forward.
- Watch out for should-ing not only yourself but also others and situations.
- Gain clarity on what's motivating your shoulds to reclaim your power.
- If your goal is truly important to *you*, you won't quit.
- Instead of should-ing others, flip your focus—find the opportunity in the challenge!
- Navigate swamps with: Empathy, Acceptance, Optimize. We all have our turn in the muck. How you choose to respond is what matters most.

ESSENTIAL #6

LEVEL UP TO GRATITUDE-BASED THINKING

*Gratitude is, first and foremost,
a way of seeing that alters our gaze.*

—Dr. Robert A. Emmons[1]

A while back, I had a client named Olivia who was a talented journalist. I saw her for several months before she moved away from Boston. But years later, she showed up again on my office doorstep—and she was quite changed. When we first worked together, she had been wrestling with classic high-achiever challenges like work stress, vexing interpersonal relationships, self-doubt, and burnout. I remember we spent many sessions working through the anxiety she felt about taking time off work for a vacation.

When she came back to treatment, her circumstances and, thus, the focus of her flashlight had shifted dramatically: Her significant other was sick. Seriously sick. And as she took her turn in a deep and unrelenting swamp, she found that, suddenly, her partner's health had become top priority. Arguably, the *only* priority. Those old worries over what her boss would think about her taking PTO or what to say in her out-of-office message were gone.

"Life is the only thing that matters," she said to me, her eyes flooding.

This incredibly difficult turn of events had inspired a seismic perspective check in her. Even in the midst of dealing with these challenges, Olivia appreciated the way it had changed her worldview. And that openness—her willingness to recognize how adversity affords us growth and the way our situation can change on a dime—allowed her to feel appreciation for every moment in her life.

Olivia couldn't escape the reality of what was happening. Of course, she had terribly challenging moments when she felt overwhelm and sadness. But she didn't feel hopeless. She knew she could wade through the swamp with as much social support and self-support as possible. And that allowed her to maintain her workload, too, despite the difficulty.

In turning *should*s to *can*s, we talked about bolstering ourselves during swampy times with Empathy, Acceptance, Optimize (or EAO). Now you've graduated from that step to one that's even more advanced—and it's all about gratitude.

I know, I know, I can practically feel you rolling your eyes again. Many high achievers think of gratitude as "soft" and they don't put much stock in it, in part because, much like taking time for self-care, it feels unproductive and even unrealistic. The ROI feels too abstract.

I promise this isn't some woo-woo or Pollyanna ideal in which I ask you to be thankful for bad things that happen. We are *not* here to practice toxic positivity. When my patients are knee-deep in miserable, murky swamps, do I look at them and say, "Now, let us be grateful for this swamp!"? No. Definitely not. That's not helpful. But if a person in the midst of a heart-wrenching struggle looks at me on their own and says, "This swamp sucks, Dr. A, but I really do believe something good will come from it," then I just validate the heck out of that thought. Because I really believe it, too.

If you want to maintain success and self-confidence even during difficult times (which we both know you do!), finding the possibility within the challenge is your ace in the hole. As Albert Einstein said, "In the middle of difficulty lies opportunity."

The swamps of life are inevitable. And self-critical high achievers can especially struggle with giving themselves the grace and kindness they need and deserve in order to thrive in hard moments. But if we can navigate these hardships with an overarching eye toward gratitude, then we can temper our anxiety, stress, and exhaustion—and actually expand and grow.

WHAT IS GRATITUDE, ANYWAY?

Gratitude has been defined in many ways. But one of my favorite takes is from research professor and author Brené Brown, PhD, MSW, who said in her number one *New York Times* bestselling book *Atlas of the Heart*: "Gratitude is an emotion that reflects our deep appreciation for what we value, what brings meaning to our lives, and what makes us feel connected to ourselves and others."[2]

I often say: Gratitude is the highest elevation of self-talk. It helps us focus our attention on appreciating things. Have you ever felt sad or angry and taken a walk? And then suddenly, out of the blue, you saw a beautiful cardinal or heard a child laughing and thought, "Maybe life isn't all bad"? Maybe your job is stressful, but you really appreciate your thoughtful coworkers. That's gratitude! Taking a moment to notice something meaningful, even as you navigate a funk. It's looking at what *is* working instead of what isn't, which helps things look less catastrophically awful so you don't fall into hopelessness and despair. Gratitude's superpower is that it grounds us in the moment, gives us perspective, and lets us start from reality. It's a direct way to overcome all three distortions in the Troublesome Trifecta in one fell swoop, and that's why it's so foundational to these 8 Essentials. Gratitude is a powerful propellant for achieving your success without being burdened by extra anxiety and stress.

DEBUNKING THE GRATITUDE MYTH

We're often socialized to believe that success comes first, then happiness (because of the success), and *then* gratitude (because we are so thankful for our happiness). But that's entirely backward! In fact, it's a widespread phenomenon I like to refer to as the Gratitude Myth, suggesting that appreciation is merely a by-product of achievement. High achievers have been taught this in spades, often without even realizing it! As a result, when I bring up gratitude, my patients often shoot me less-than-enthusiastic smiles. "Dr. A, that's really *sweet* and all, but I just don't have time to write a letter to my past professor telling him that his class is what made me decide to go after my dream." Or, "How is saying thank you to a store clerk really going to make any difference in my trajectory or theirs?" By "sweet," of course, they mean weak, unimportant, naive. I get it—saying thank you (or practicing gratitude in any other number of ways) will indeed use up some of your time and energy. And the correlation between appreciation and career success, overall excellence, and joy may at first be difficult to grasp, beyond the theoretical. That's especially true for high achievers, who see success as the primary goal. Why would you put anything else first?

WHICH COMES FIRST: THE HAPPINESS OR THE GRATITUDE?

The answer can be found in that Gratitude Myth to which we're so attached. If we flip it on its head, where do we land? I'd posit that, as surprising as it may seem, the real, accurate equation is this:

GRATITUDE ⟹ HAPPINESS ⟹ SUCCESS

Yep! That's for real. Remember: Gratitude is a high level of self-talk. And what do our thoughts impact? Our feelings (happiness) and behaviors or outcomes (success). Many, many studies have shown that gratitude is associated with a multitude of benefits, ranging from lower stress levels to improved sleep quality and social relationships.[3] And we know by now how important lowering stress, enacting foundational self-care like consistent sleep, and cultivating healthy relationships are to escaping burnout for our maintainable success. In his book *Gratitude Works*, Dr. Robert Emmons, a premier researcher on the topic, describes gains for diverse participants in a variety of studies including:

- Increased feelings of energy, alertness, enthusiasm, and vigor
- Success in achieving personal goals
- Bolstered feelings of self-worth and self-confidence
- Greater sense of purpose and resilience

And those profound benefits are not amorphous or theoretical. They're statistically concrete. According to Emmons's book,[4] people who keep gratitude journals, one of the most common practices for increasing appreciation, are 25 percent happier, exercise 33 percent more each week, and sleep thirty minutes more per night. And as we know, factors such as physical activity, sleep, and happiness are core tenets of career momentum! Kind of like the opposite of feeling defeated.

In his TED Talk, Benedictine monk and author David Steindl-Rast asks us to think about the people we know in our lives who seem to have everything they need but are still unhappy, and then to think about the people we know who represent the reverse. Gratitude is not about what you have; it's about *valuing* what you have. From this, he draws a related connection: "So, it is not happiness that makes us grateful,"

Steindl-Rast asserts. "It's gratefulness that makes us happy."[5] Basically, the experts agree: Don't wait to feel happy to start being thankful for things! The secret is to start with gratitude.

Just as Dr. Brené Brown referenced, gratitude connects us to what is authentically meaningful to us. It means focusing our flashlight on something good or valuable in our lives, inspiring more balanced thoughts. Thankfulness keeps our thoughts, feelings, and behaviors on a more positive, productive track, which makes us feel good about ourselves and the world.

HAPPINESS BEGETS SUCCESS

As a high achiever, you're probably thinking, "Yeah, fine. Happiness is great. But what about my success?" Fair enough. But guess what—as we've touched on before, happiness fuels success! Yep, say it again. Shout it from the rooftops. Make it your screensaver. Remember, as author Shawn Achor said in *The Happiness Advantage*, "cultivating positive brains makes us more motivated, efficient, resilient, creative, and productive, which drives performance upward."[6] I have seen this play out countless times in my own office, as well. Happiness means having the energy, wherewithal, and creative confidence to ascend. It signals balanced thinking, a charged battery, and a strong sense of self-worth, which means less unmanaged anxiety and more forward motion toward your highest goals. And once we come to understand this, it seems simple enough that happiness and success would be connected, despite being antithetical to what we understand culturally about climbing the career ladder. In fact, we have all experienced this at one time or another, even just a day when we wake up with strong mojo, looking and feeling good, ready to take on the workday and make strides in our lives. When we arrive at the office with good ideas and great coworker banter and are just crushing it. We know what it feels like to have happiness propel us toward other positive outcomes.

Gratitude equals happiness, which equals success, because thankful *thoughts* help you *feel* better and *behave* as your best self.

GRATITUDE AND THE TROUBLESOME TRIFECTA

So how to translate your gratitude into happiness? Thankfully (pun totally intended), appreciation has the power to help you balance your unhelpful thoughts, which—as we now know—is the key to healthy self-talk. That means less anxiety and worry—and more happiness. Ultimately, gratitude is a practical tool you can use to your benefit. Let's take a look at how it can combat each distortion in the Troublesome Trifecta.

Thank You ... To Mitigate All-or-Nothing Thinking

As a reminder, All-or-Nothing Thinking is when, instead of allowing for nuance or gradations, we find ourselves expressing our concerns through absolutes and extremes, using words like "always," "everyone," and "never." Everything is black or white.

Conversely, gratitude ushers in the gray. Say you've had a bad day and, as you ready to walk home in the cold, you find yourself thinking, "Everything is terrible!" Bringing in gratitude would allow you to notice some things that are maybe okay or even good. It could be something small like the fact that your cozy coat is keeping you warm despite poor weather or that you have an episode of a favorite TV show cued up and waiting at home. It just has to be enough for you to realize not *everything* is *completely* ruined. You're not a *total* failure. Gratitude helps you find positive and meaningful things on which to train your flashlight so you can genuinely say, "I do have this good thing." In this way, it helps you access a more accurate view and identify evidence to use to poke holes in unhelpful thoughts. And then, by using that evidence to develop new and improved self-talk, you defeat the all-or-nothing distortion. In other words, gratitude = perspective. It can allow you to think, "Okay. Maybe it was just an unfortunate day. And maybe I can even enjoy the few hours left."

Being grateful is not about trying to force silver linings in an avoidant or minimizing way. This isn't about telling yourself, "Other people have it way harder than I do, so I'm being spoiled and am not entitled to feel upset." Don't self-shame by saying, "It could be worse." Don't use gratitude against yourself or others! After all, that's just another thing about which to feel bad, another way to beat yourself up. And gratitude is also not a method for avoiding reality. For example, I wouldn't encourage my recently unemployed patient Keith to focus solely on peripheral positives in order to avoid confronting his situation.

Practicing gratitude is about concretely engaging with what is—which is another way of saying that gratitude is all about approach instead of avoidance. And it's accessible! It's a tool that is always available to you. To bring more of it into your life, you just have to practice it. So for Keith, I'd suggest mitigating the negative thoughts he has about himself in the wake of losing his position—"I'm such a loser and I'm never going to get another job"—by focusing on three to five things he appreciates about himself and his life. These act as concrete evidence that he is not "such a loser" and take the air right out of that all-or-nothing balloon. The gratitude-based spin might be: "I am grateful I worked hard and graduated from a great university; I am grateful I have friends who care about me and who I can talk to; and I am grateful I have enough in savings to pay my bills while I continue my job search." By focusing his attention on what he has to be grateful for, Keith can generate the more helpful thoughts: "I feel stressed and disappointed that I lost my job, but I'm not necessarily a loser because I got laid off. I have so many things in my life I am grateful for."

Keith is definitely *not* a "loser." He just has something important to figure out. And thanks to gratitude, now he's better poised to face challenges instead of feeling defeated in advance and perhaps creating a self-fulfilling prophecy.

Appreciation is higher ground. It provides a much better vantage point than avoidance or All-or-Nothing Thinking.

Thank You... To Overcome Jumping to Conclusions

At this point, you're now well versed in how Jumping to Conclusions depletes your energy and makes you worry your way into the future. We care so much about the outcome that we often spiral into what-ifs and worrying about what will happen, even assuming the worst and becoming riddled with anxiety in advance. But if we can root ourselves in gratitude, that's a different story! Remember when I was in the Florida car rental place at the airport and I started freaking out for fear that I wouldn't know where to go, instead of trusting myself to figure it out? All because I was actually nervous about my job interview?

What if I had slowed down for a second to be grateful that the airline didn't lose my luggage or that the rental company had a nice car ready for me to rent? If I had just stayed grateful in that moment, how different would I have felt? What if I had appreciated that I was in warm Florida instead of cold Boston with a plush hotel room waiting for me? I was so in my head that I wasn't enjoying the moment I was in, even though, in retrospect, it was a really good, exciting moment!

Gratitude will give you the gifts of perspective and energy in the present, which will empower you as you move forward. I may have been thinking, "What if I mess up the interview and don't get the job?" Think about how this self-talk would impact my mood and vibrancy. Now, what if I transformed it with gratitude? "I really hope I get the job, but either way I'm excited and grateful I got the interview. I'm thankful I'll gain interviewing experience and get to soak up some sunshine." Remember how in Essential #3, we practiced getting excited about opportunity? Well, this is how you level up! You layer in gratitude.

> **The Takeaway:** If you strategically focus your thoughts on appreciating meaningful or positive aspects of your present

moment, instead of wasting your energy erroneously making assumptions about the unknown, you will have a powerful advantage. Your thinking will be more balanced, which will help you feel more stable, confident, and invigorated—so you'll navigate uncertainty and ambiguity more successfully.

Thank You... To Slay Should Statements

Gratitude encourages you to appreciate how you, others, and situations actually *are* rather than needlessly inciting anxiety and distress by focusing on how you think reality *should* be different. It allows you to be aware of—and thankful for—what is in front of you instead of ruminating about what isn't. It inspires you to focus on what's working in your life.

So you can overcome should-ing yourself by focusing on what you are grateful for about your life rather than what you are lacking. Here's a common scenario:

> **The Situation:** You set a goal to go to sleep by 10:00 p.m. last night, but you actually went to bed at 11:30 p.m.
> **The Should:** I *should* have gone to bed by 10:00 p.m. What's wrong with me? I should be able to complete my goals.
> **The Gratitude Reframe:** I'm grateful that I care about my self-care enough to set goals to improve my sleep habits. I'm grateful that tonight will be another opportunity to go to bed earlier. I'm grateful I know it's okay to rework my goals and that, if 10:00 p.m. isn't doable yet, I'll set my goal to be in bed by 11:00 p.m. tonight—I can do that!

At first it might feel awkward to self-talk in this way, but the more you do it, the more organic gratitude-based thinking will become.

This type of elevated self-talk can also help you overcome your habit of should-ing others. Our existing toolbox includes strategies for accepting others by flipping our focus and recognizing what others *do* contribute, à la Essential #5. But now you're ready to level up. That's right! You've done the work. You're ready to begin actually *appreciating* the positive aspects you've identified in others and the opportunities they provide to learn and grow. For example:

The Situation: You received an assignment back from your professor (or perhaps a proposal back from your boss) covered with comments—about the need for proper punctuation, how to enhance clarity, and the importance of spell-check.

The Should: My professor shouldn't be so hard on me. And I should have done better!

The Gratitude Reframe: I'm grateful my professor is giving his time and energy to offer specific feedback about my work, which I can use to become a better writer.

TAKE ACTION

Let's try the Gratitude Reframe on for size! First, think of a situation that you could reframe. Start with a mild occasion in which you should-ed yourself or should-ed others.

The Situation:

The Should:

The Gratitude Reframe:

Practice reframing your unbalanced thoughts!

How did doing this Take Action make you feel? Over time, if you practice the Gratitude Reframe regularly, you'll notice that your thoughts and feelings start to shift, which will also improve your behaviors.

So, you've learned how to overcome should-ing yourself and others. Now we need to learn how gratitude-based thinking can help you overcome should-ing situations.

FINDING GRATITUDE IN THE SWAMPS

Of course, finding a way to feel gratitude isn't always easy, as helpful as it can be. It's all well and good to say that this leveled-up self-talk can make a big difference. But how do we identify moments of opportunity? We use the swamps as fuel. In my experience, there are three advantages within the swamps of life that come up again and again and are ideal to pinpoint when trying to inspire your own gratitude-based thinking: perspective, courage, and growth. These three strengths will help you not only in the swamp but throughout your life afterward as well. They make meaning from muck.

Appreciate All Things

Yes, it is possible and even beneficial to acknowledge with gratitude the good that comes from your swamps. Again, that does *not* mean you have to be grateful for a hardship! It means that, if you can find the opportunity amid the muck and mire, the swamp is less likely to keep you stuck. In sessions, I introduce this concept of how to recognize the possibilities within difficult situations delicately, because I never want to minimize someone's challenges or experiences. But I introduce it nonetheless, because otherwise I know I'm not helping my patients as much as I could. If you are suffering, we are gonna find a way to use it. Make it be in the service of something greater, give it a sense of purpose. Because any swamp you've survived is part of the journey that brought you to where you are today, to this very moment. They've endowed you with insights, understanding, character, and sometimes even drive. For better or worse, as we've acknowledged, swamps are where we learn some of our most important life lessons.

American essayist, poet, and philosopher Ralph Waldo Emerson similarly encouraged: "Cultivate the habit of being grateful for every good thing that comes to you, and to give thanks continuously. And because all things have contributed to your advancement, you should include all things in your gratitude."

All things. Because it really is the truth that each and every experience of your life has made you who you are today. And you are valuable exactly as you are.

So, since changes and challenges are inevitable, it's adaptive to integrate them into your bigger picture. The alternative is to dishonor your times spent in the swamps by perceiving them as useless or disconnected from your growth as a person. What if you consider making your way through a swamp a success in itself, an achievement from which you learned and for which you could feel proud?

For example, my patients who ache after recent romantic breakups often later say that although they felt distressed during their post-dumped days, it allowed them the space to find much better matches for themselves. I've also worked with many patients with cancer who report they would absolutely never have chosen to get cancer, of course, but found that it gave them a new, deeper understanding of what's actually important in life and an ability to not sweat the small stuff.

I experienced this for myself when I was thirteen years old. My great-aunt Peg from Scotland had gifted me an old waterbed that I loved. One night, while my parents were away on a rare trip, its faulty wiring started an electrical fire. That night, our house burned down. We lost everything we owned, except my school backpack that a thoughtful firefighter had saved by tossing it out an open window onto the grass. Of course, the experience was deeply upsetting and scary. But when my parents returned, they modeled a kind of gratitude that set the tone for my perspective. My older brother Johnny had noticed an odd smell in my room before the fire and had me sleep elsewhere. He was also the person who alerted us all when the smoke detectors woke him.

"He's a hero," they said. "We are so blessed."

"Blessed?" I wondered. I had just lost almost all of my earthly possessions.

"Yes," my mother explained, "because no one was hurt." That was a defining moment in my life. Ever since, I have known in a profound way that all that matters is people.

Was I grateful for the fire? For losing all my favorite stuffed animals and photo albums? My favorite clothes? Are my patients grateful for the heartache and the cancer? For their pain? Their suffering? Oh, heck no. We're not here to romanticize that. Gratitude isn't about forcing ourselves to paste a fake smile on our face while we're hurting. It's about being open to and appreciative of the discoveries found inside these difficult moments. As gratitude expert David Steindl-Rast said, people don't have to "be grateful for everything... [but] we can be grateful in every given moment for the opportunity."[7]

While it may feel challenging, the truth is that you will benefit tremendously from choosing to focus on being grateful for how your swamp is actually a *setup*—rather than a *setback*—for something more. It's the secret to managing your mood and moving yourself forward when you are feeling anxious, overwhelmed, and stuck in a nasty bog. Sometimes it takes awhile to get there, though. And that's okay, too. It's a process of learning to find opportunity in the muck.

Earned Courage

In addition to perspective, courage is earned in the swamp. That's another element we can look for and acknowledge as we try to encourage our own gratitude-based thinking. When we traverse those unpleasant marshlands of life, we gain invaluable dimension and depth. Again, adversity helps us evolve and transition into the next-level version of ourselves. I often tell my patients, "The 'Disneyland days' of life are important—to relax and enjoy fun moments—but those are not the ones that will make you stronger or help you grow as a person." Many a patient has nodded in agreement: "Yep, this feels like the cosmic consolation prize, Dr. A." They recognize that certain wisdom and insights are learned only in the swamps.

Understanding this is another facet of gratitude-based thinking. Courage, quite simply, is earned from experience. To be clear, that doesn't mean never feeling scared. Being frightened in the face of uncertainty—job loss, grief, illness, a life plan getting derailed or not working out as we'd imagined—is natural. So don't start beating yourself up for it, no matter how much your high-achieving tendencies try to inundate you with self-criticism! Courage means persevering despite your fear or heartache. And once you survive a swamp, however difficult, you know that you can face adversity, so you'll feel less anxious when confronted with challenging situations. This is an idea that can help spur gratitude-based thinking, because it reminds us that there's something to be gained. As Eleanor Roosevelt famously said, "You gain strength, courage, and confidence by every experience in which you really stop to look fear in the face. You are able to say to yourself, 'I have lived through this horror. I can take the next thing that comes along.'"

Growth Factor

In recent years, we as a culture have become more familiar with the concept of PTSD, or post-traumatic stress disorder. But most people have not heard of PTG, because it's a less discussed alternative outcome to trauma. Post-traumatic growth (PTG) is the "positive psychological change experienced as a result of the struggle with highly challenging life circumstances."[8] Like fresh perspective and courage, knowing about PTG helps my patients recognize that, while they may experience distress as a result of trauma or dramatic changes in their lives, there is another, more beneficial outcome that can sometimes occur, as well: growth.

According to cognitive scientist Dr. Scott Barry Kaufman, PTG can help "turn adversity into advantage." Areas of growth related to coping with adversity include "greater appreciation of life, greater appreciation and strengthening of close relationships, increased compassion and altruism, the identification of new possibilities or a purpose in life, greater awareness and utilization of personal strengths, enhanced spiritual development, [and] creative growth."[9] So, not only can coping with adversity make you a stronger person, but it can also potentially propel you toward new goals in life, new passions, and new ambitions. Often it is after people gain perspective via difficult situations that they finally find their calling. And of course, once you're doing work that speaks to your authentic passions, the sky's the limit!

"It is precisely when the foundational structure of the self is shaken that we are in the best position to pursue new opportunities in our lives," explains Dr. Kaufman.[10] There's a fascinating reality that we can achieve more success after having been through the swamp than we would have if we hadn't struggled at all. These challenging experiences put us in the best position to take advantage of the perspective and opportunities that appear before us.

Knowing about PTG can give you hope.[11] It offers something for which to feel gratitude on dark days. And you can harness the immense power of hope during your swampiest moments. Use it to empower you. Remind yourself that you really can turn your challenges into advantages. And that you can, as I tell patients, transform your burns into benevolence. This will help you face the realities of what's coming with more confidence and less fear, turning to action instead of avoidance.

Find ways to use the difficulties you've endured to benefit others, too. It will energize you. And keep you moving forward.

TAKE ACTION

When you look back at difficult moments in your life, what helped you get through to the other side? If you're wading through a swamp right now, what's helping you out? One way to incorporate more gratitude is to acknowledge and appreciate what or who helps pull you through. Focus on self-reflection about your own hard-earned lessons in your swamp. There's a wide range of what bolsters us in our most challenging moments. What does it for you? An upbeat TV show? A certain album? A delicious and convenient local restaurant? A kind mail carrier who shoots you a daily smile? Or maybe a family member or friend who checks in, makes you laugh, or brings you treats to show they care? You learn who stands by you in the swamps. Ask yourself:

- What cheered me up? What gave me moments of joy?
- What or who made me feel comforted and understood?
- Who were the people who were with me? Who had my back?
- In what ways did they concretely help me?
- What would have been different without them there?

Take a moment and be grateful for what these people or experiences gave you!

THANK YOU, MAUI

Now that we know what to look for to spark our gratitude, even in the swamps, I want to share a concrete tool that you can use to boost your experience of gratitude in your daily life. There are a million great practices for kick-starting gratitude, from journaling to meditating and more. People even make gratitude trees, giving thanks on each leaf! I personally write down five things for which I am grateful every night before I go to sleep.

During the day, though, my go-to is a relaxation-appreciation mash-up I call Thank You, Maui, which blends the stress management technique of visual imagery[12] with a focus on gratitude to activate your awareness and appreciation of a special, meaningful place you value. According to Cleveland Clinic, guided imagery pulls you out of a stressful moment and allows you to calm the body and mind. Benefits include slowed breathing and heart rate, improved sleep, reduced anxiety and depression, and even decreased pain![13]

For our purposes, the environment you imagine can be anywhere you find peaceful and gratitude-promoting. A beach, a forest, a backyard peppered with Adirondack chairs, a park on a summer evening, even a restaurant with twinkle lights overlooking the water—somewhere you want to remember. My place is Maui, one of the most gorgeous spots I've ever visited. When I'm there in my mind, I think of lush landscapes, serene quiet, sweet shaved ice, the salty smell of the Pacific, listening to the rhythmic sounds of the ocean, and feeling warm sand squish beneath my toes. Beautiful. When I visited, I recall it being profoundly soothing to sit on the beach under an umbrella and watch the azure waves roll in, one after the other. When will I return to Maui? I'm honestly not sure. But I know that just by closing my eyes, I can feel Maui's calming vibes and be grateful for my memories of it—every day if I want to. No flight necessary.

The place you choose is ideally somewhere you've actually been before and associate with feeling relaxed so that you can more easily picture the scene and connect back to the sensations of being there. It's a spot that you appreciate having had the opportunity to enjoy—even if it's just your backyard. Some patients choose to visualize being on scenic trails in the woods they are thankful to have walked, gazing at snow-covered mountains through the windows of a cozy winter cabin, or curling up in their treasured comfy reading nook at home.

Close your eyes and let your mind wander over memories of verdant fields, enchanting forests, blooming gardens, bright-blue sky over vast ocean, favorite vacation spots. Places of tranquility. What is your happy place?

Once you've chosen *your* Maui, identify the details there as they connect to each of your five senses. Ask yourself: What do I see? What do I hear? What do I smell? What do I taste? What do I touch? This is what you'll be using during your visualization.

TAKE ACTION: GOING TO YOUR MAUI IN YOUR MIND

Now it's time to visit *your* gratitude- and peace-enhancing place. Practice first during a moment when you're only somewhat or minimally stressed so you can get used to visualizing and eventually use it when your anxiety is higher, as well.

1. Find a quiet, distraction-free place and turn off your electronics—even if it's just for a few minutes.
2. Begin to bring on the calm: Close your eyes and breathe in deeply through your nose for a count of 4 and then exhale slowly through your mouth for a count of 6. Repeat three times or more.
3. Go to your happy place in your mind. Spend some time savoring your cherished location. Remember to focus on your five senses—what you see, hear, smell, taste, and touch. Soak it all in!
4. Recognize as your tension lessens and your body begins to feel more relaxed. Enjoy sinking into this restfulness as you continue picturing the details of your treasured place.

5. Exhale slowly and open your eyes. Notice feeling calm, content, and grateful. Focus on how thankful you are to have this memory to come back to. Realize that not everyone has had the opportunity to experience such a special, pleasant place. Think about how you've benefited from being able to visit and then visualize this place. Appreciate how relaxation and gratitude feel. Out loud or in your mind, say, "I am grateful for [your Maui]."

When you're feeling frustrated or anxious or are navigating a swampy moment and need a gratitude infusion to help you approach what's next with more ease, you can take as long or short of a time exploring your imagined, soothing scenario as you'd like. You don't have to wait until things feel bad. Many patients regularly find quiet spots to sit during lunch breaks or at the end of the day to get centered by focusing on their version of Maui.

Visual imagery alone is not going to eliminate all of your overwhelm. But it can take tension down a notch, especially when you call it in as a quick, convenient way to relax between tasks—a great ROI on a few minutes of quiet while you're stuck at your desk or the weather is dreary and you can't get outside. Going to Maui in your mind certainly beats scrolling through other people's pictures of Maui on social!

This relaxation-gratitude enhancer is especially helpful for hardworking strivers, who get more easily sucked into the daily grind, perseverating on what-ifs and trying to perfect even the minutiae of every work project. Thank You, Maui, can free you up to take a moment for yourself, refocus your energy on somewhere meaningful to you, and feel refreshed.

After all, once you're able to access gratitude, it can be infused into every part of your life. There's no downside. In our hardest moments, as our thoughts spiral, and even in our lighter times when we want to pause and acknowledge the good in our lives, appreciation can make us feel good about ourselves and the world. It can make us happy. Which equals success.

As author Haruki Murakami wrote in his beloved novel *Kafka on the Shore*, "And once the storm is over, you won't remember how you made it through, how you managed to survive. You won't even be sure whether the storm is really over. But one thing is certain. When you come out of the storm, you won't be the same person who walked in."[14] In fact, we emerge as people with new strengths, depth, and understanding. And for that, we are truly grateful.

TOP TAKEAWAYS

- **GRATITUDE** ➡ **HAPPINESS** ➡ **SUCCESS**—not the other way around!
- If we practice gratitude-based thinking in our toughest moments, we can navigate them with less anxiety and more ease.
- Lessons are learned and courage is earned in the swamps.
- When you need a quick, convenient minute or two of gratitude and calm, go to your Maui in your mind.

ESSENTIAL #7

CELEBRATE THE VICTORIES

Never, ever underestimate the importance of having fun.

—Randy Pausch

Imagine that you're summiting Kilimanjaro. You've been hiking for days, training for months before that, envisioning this moment perhaps for years. You finally reach the top. You're surrounded by crystal blue skies, buoyant clouds, sleek white snow reflecting sunlight. You're literally on top of the world. What do you do? Do you shrug your shoulders and start walking back down? Or do you take a long look around to appreciate the view you worked so hard to see?

Taking that moment to celebrate—or bask in the glow of your success—is more important than you might imagine. At first it might seem almost self-indulgent to consciously let that win sink in, to take the extra beat to say, "Wow. I just reached this summit." To breathe the crisp air, take a seat, and drink some water, eat a snack. But actually, celebrating means making the time to give thanks. It means pausing to acknowledge and actively appreciate achieving a desired outcome. And we know from Essential #6 how important appreciation and gratitude can be—not just for your own sense of accomplishment but also for all the people and opportunities that made it possible. You learned how to make your way through swamps. Now you get to navigate your path through victories.

TAKE SOME TIME TO CELEBRATE!

Celebrating wins is crucial because, ultimately, acknowledging successes helps you overcome cognitive distortions, boosts your energy and mood, and advances future achievements. You may recall that when you've identified cognitive distortions throughout this book, I've been encouraging you to pat yourself on the back for having caught them. But why? How does donning a party hat and toasting with champagne flutes move you forward? As psychologist and author of *Hardwiring Happiness*, Rick Hanson, PhD, explains, "Your brain is like Velcro for negative experiences but Teflon for positive ones."[1] As we've touched on before, the human brain has a hardwired negativity bias, which makes us more likely to intake and focus on negative experiences rather than on positive ones. If we don't intentionally take a moment to log a positive experience—or mindfully snap a literal or mental picture of a success—we're likely to lose both the specific details of the memory and, perhaps even more important, the fulfilling feeling of having reached a goal. And just as we return to our "Maui" to recall and feel a sense of relaxation, it's incredibly important that we hold tight to our wins to use as powerful, encouraging reminders when we are climbing the next mountain. Pausing at the peak, so to speak, and taking the time to revel in a completed task is critical because it's what will help you strategically "take in the good" and defeat your brain's bias of dwelling on the negative.[2] This is what will keep you focused, pumped up, and believing in yourself as you ascend to the next summit.

Keep in mind that a celebration doesn't have to be anything huge or extravagant, unless you want it to be! It can simply be those moments you take for yourself to intentionally pause to honor what you—and the team of people who also contributed to the victory—accomplished. A celebration can take any form that feels fun or meaningful to you. Some of my favorite possibilities:

- **Traditional.** Go for a special dinner or gathering with teammates, friends, family—whoever aided the win. Sing, dance, be merry!
- **Gift.** Select yourself an item that will remind you of your success in the future—anything from a postcard to a piece of jewelry engraved with the date. Any lasting symbol of the achievement as a keepsake or reward.
- **Personal.** Take time to commemorate your triumph—detail it in your journal or go to a peaceful place and think about how wonderful it is that your time and effort transformed your ideas into a real victory!
- **Adventure.** Go do something you've never done before—*finally* take the trip you've always imagined, try out horseback riding, go for a hot-air balloon ride, explore unknown places and activities.
- **Pay it forward.** Harness the positive energy from your win to help others: Volunteer at a community event, donate clothes to a local charity, write a letter of gratitude to someone who helped you on your journey, or sign up to be a mentor and encourage others to achieve their goals.

However you choose to honor the victories, know that both big and small wins lead you to achieving your greatest goals.

WHERE'S THE PARTY?

Celebrating can be easy—and even joyful! And yet despite our understanding of the importance of pausing and the fact that it's fun, this step is too often skipped in our culture. "Individuals and organizations tend to have an 'on-to-the-next' mindset, as though it is contrary to productivity and efficiency to relish, even briefly, reaching our objectives," notes author and CEO Whitney Johnson in her *Harvard Business Review* article "Celebrate to Win." "Nothing could be further from the truth. Celebration is an important opportunity to cement the lessons learned on the path to achievement, and to strengthen the relationships between people that make future achievement more plausible."[3] Constantly moving on to the next without pausing to notice a goal met is a fast track to burnout and robs us of vital recovery and refuel/self-care time.

Skipping the celebration also cheats us out of logging the positive experience in our memory, which is so beneficial. "In most cases, we don't consistently and systematically take the extra seconds to *install* these experiences in the brain," explains Rick Hanson, PhD.[4] The author offers three steps for "taking in the good." First, you notice an experience, person, or completed task about which you feel positive or grateful. Second, continue focusing on that experience "for five to ten seconds or longer," thinking about how it's meaningful to you and staying open to the feelings it evokes. Third, let it truly sink in and know that the experience is now an asset inside of you.[5] In other words, to turn a passing positive moment into a long-term memory—to essentially download it to our brains like an app that we can benefit from and return to regularly for a boost—takes only seconds of our time and attention.

Ask yourself: Are you shining your light on what you've accomplished? Or on what's next? We have to train ourselves to pay attention to our achievements.

In an unfortunate twist, celebrating remains especially challenging for high achievers. But why? We achieve great things! That's quite literally what makes us high achievers! We set goals, meet them, and excel all over the place. It's built right into the name! But the achievements themselves fall to the wayside.

This is a major problem. After all, high achievers who don't make time to celebrate are missing out on the potential to use their victories as a powerfully positive source of social connection, learning, and mood-boosting pleasure, as well as concrete reminders to increase confidence and motivation. So why not celebrate? Well, it comes back to the thorny Troublesome Trifecta and related issues.

Jumping to Conclusions

As always, high achievers are resistant to taking a break, so focused on the outcome that they're afraid to take their eyes off the prize for even a moment. Tumbling down that deep Negative Fortune-Telling hole, they often assume, with mounting anxiety, that taking time off to celebrate will cause them to lose their momentum or fall behind. This erroneous belief is further fueled by social comparison. After all, you don't frequently see people celebrating small progress wins on Instagram. Instead of discussing the many steps involved in arriving at a major goal, people post about their biggest accomplishments, so we assume that they're effortlessly flitting from giant win to giant win.

Celebrating small victories isn't something that's modeled in our culture, in general. Not by parents, teachers, businesses, or universities. So, high achievers have often never observed this practice. And their innate desire to keep up with or outdo others moves them to predict negatively about celebrating. Instead of staying curious and considering how marking a win could be beneficial, they worry it will slow them down. Their fervent belief that they always need to keep pushing forward leads them to think that taking a moment to acknowledge success will put them at a severe disadvantage. Which leads us to All-or-Nothing Thinking…

All-or-Nothing Thinking

If you're an anxious high achiever prone to cognitive distortions like the Troublesome Trifecta, you may find yourself digging into the narrative that your success doesn't count if it isn't perfect. Who cares if you climbed Kilimanjaro if it took you extra time or you needed a bit of help? Or if you couldn't get to the very top because of weather conditions? It's as if you never had any success at all! Also related, many of my anxious high-achieving patients who are bogged down in All-or-Nothing Thinking only acknowledge long-term goals instead of celebrating milestones along the way. "Dr. A, I'll celebrate when I'm done!" they assure me.

In grad school, the only reasonable goal is graduation, never mind doing well on a big exam or paper. At work, it's a promotion or huge new job. For high achievers, the smaller wins may not seem special enough to celebrate. Often my patients have accomplished many goals—won awards, had their articles published, been accepted into important groups, been honored in various ways—so they get desensitized to the achievements. Wins that *deserve* to be celebrated.

In truth, most excellent achievements take time—earning degrees, publishing books, earning tenure, making partner at a law firm—and if you wait to celebrate, you're really missing out on so many important markers along the way that are huge accomplishments in themselves and could be converted into fuel for success.

Should-ing (Yes, It's Back!)

Just as with taking breaks for self-care, high achievers often believe that taking time to celebrate is "lazy" or will make them lose their edge and settle for mediocrity. They tell themselves they should keep working instead of acknowledging the win. Instead of using achievements as natural pauses for recovery time (and dumping Gatorade over people's metaphorical heads just as elite athletes do after winning a championship), high achievers grind themselves into a should-spiral burnout. In the same way they jump to conclusions about falling behind, they mistake a pause for paralysis—or fear that a break will bring that on. They don't understand that the pause to celebrate is strategic. That it's actually necessary to pause to *keep* their edge and be able to optimally achieve their next big goal! "We get trapped into thinking that if we're not always working hard, we'll be surpassed by the competition," write Brad Stulberg and Steve Magness in their book *Peak Performance*. But they go on to say, "Studies show that vigor and performance increase following a rest day."[6]

We feel we *should* keep working—especially when we're very busy—when in fact taking time to stop and acknowledge our success is what will propel us forward toward excellence. So just as we did with self-care, we need to schedule our celebrations. Put them in your calendar the way you would a party for a friend. Prioritize them, even when other demands come up—'cause they will. Lock them down! Remember: Your celebration can be as simple as a ten-minute walk in which you bask in the glow of meeting your goal.

Wavering Self-Worth

It's also important to question what's underlying your goals: If your root motivation is about trying to prove yourself or be seen as lovable by others, you're setting yourself up for chronic disappointment, because no amount of achievement is ever going to fill that void. This is what prompts high achievers to constantly move their goalposts, creating new objectives just as the previous one is being realized and before taking time to rejoice in it. They want to keep achieving so they feel special, valuable, "enough." But no accomplishment will actually ever satisfy this because it's based on faulty thinking, trying to substantiate internal worth with external validation.

High achievers crave expansion and growth, but it's important to have balance—to take time to revel in the positives instead of amassing achievements for their own sake. We see this outward success-as-a-destination issue play out regularly with celebrities, who reach stardom only to find themselves feeling empty and hopeless. Because, ultimately, you can't earn your worth. It's crucial to know and trust your own intrinsic, unconditional value as a human being.

And what helps us honor our inherent worth? Showing ourselves that we're deserving of time and attention! That includes acknowledging and remembering our victories. Celebrating! Which is, essentially, an expression of gratitude, which makes us happy, which drives success. So, your future sustainable success depends on it! "Celebrating achievements great and small is high octane fuel for further achievement," says Johnson in her *Harvard Business Review* article. "We don't just celebrate the win; we celebrate *to* win."[7]

5 REASONS TO CELEBRATE!

Celebration is actually a strategic tool for paving the path to continued success—yep, those colorful streamers and balloons are fuel for ascension to excellence! If pausing to acknowledge the successfully completed feat foreshadows the cresting of many more mountains, why and how does it work? How specifically does pumping fists for achievements benefit you as a high achiever? Why do we need this tool?

1. *Strengthen Self-Talk*

For starters, celebrating a win bolsters your self-talk and self-confidence. After all, what feels better than taking a moment to acknowledge your own awesomeness? What boosts your self-esteem more than setting a goal and meeting it, then taking a second to think, "I did that! It was me!" Are you flexing in the mirror just thinking about it? Maybe not quite yet. But you'll get there! Celebrating a win helps you focus the light of your attention on the good in life. It spotlights concrete evidence of your capability that you can use to poke holes in unbalanced thinking.

Take, for example, my patient Allison, who spent months studying for a major exam. We worked to build self-care time into her days to help her manage her anxiety, but she still sometimes struggled with self-doubt and stress-inducing what-if self-talk. "What if I'm not studying enough? What if I don't pass?" Finally, results day came: She passed! Go, Allison! She felt relieved, naturally. But what if she took the time to celebrate that victory versus just moving on to the next exam? How might she feel? And how would her feelings then likely impact her behaviors?

Well, not only would a celebratory dinner or even a fifteen-minute victory lap around the park while listening to her favorite music make her feel proud and cement the memory in her mind, but it might also increase her confidence. According to a *Psychology Today* article by Benjamin Cheyette, MD, and Sarah Cheyette, MD, "The positive feeling you get when you succeed is what ultimately builds confidence. It builds hope that you will be successful again. When you are confident and hopeful, that improves your ability to focus naturally. When you feel that way, you are more likely to concentrate again on a challenging task in the future because you will feel motivated to get that feeling back."[8]

In other words, by celebrating passing her exam (which she did!— by taking time to write about the win in her journal while at the beach), Allison equipped herself with more swagger for when she approached the next test. This was concrete evidence of her aptitude that she could use to poke holes in her self-doubting thoughts in the future. A few months later, before her next big exam, when she began focusing on the Negative Fortune-Telling thought, "My exam definitely isn't going to go well," her new and improved self-talk shot back. "Actually, I passed my previous big exam. I thought it wouldn't go well, but it did. So I can do my best preparing for this one, too, and be hopeful that it will turn out the same way!" This type of more helpful, balanced thinking, spurred by past successes, decreases anxiety and increases motivation. Again, more helpful thoughts lead to more positive feelings and behaviors.

So, stopping and taking the time to focus on your victories through celebration helps you overcome your cognitive distortions and strengthen your self-talk, improving your mood, elevating your energy, and building momentum as you approach the next big hurdle.

2. Victory! Rinse and Repeat

You know you can learn from mistakes, but you can learn from your successes, too! This means amassing new knowledge, which moves you forward toward excellence. When you pause to appreciate your wins, you're taking time to focus on what *worked*. Ask yourself:

- Broadly, what contributed to my success?
- More specifically, what particular actions did I take or thoughts did I focus on that helped me achieve my victory?

Without this step, you'd miss out on some potentially powerful data collection! And pausing to celebrate is a positively focused or joyful way to reflect on what contributed to your success. While reflection may not always feel active or productive in an obvious way to high achievers, it's a tremendously helpful tool for gaining perspective and useful insights. Bestselling author and leadership expert John C. Maxwell writes about his own "reflective thinking" in his book *How Successful People Think*. "My goal is to reflect so that I might learn from my successes and mistakes, discover what I should try to repeat, and determine what I should change," he says. "It is always a valuable exercise."[9]

Say you just gave a super-informative and engaging presentation and won your company a big new client. By stopping to bask, you give yourself a moment to consider why it went so well: Did you get a good night's sleep the night before? Did you work tirelessly to prepare but then give yourself a break the day before? Did you structure it a certain way or present yourself in a certain light? What went right?

You may be wondering: Can't we just have a debriefing meeting where we try to ascertain this data? Sure. But here's the thing: It's not as fun. And your happiness matters. After all, as we've learned, happiness fuels success. It really is just as productive, if not more advantageous, to enjoy celebrating your victories rather than just dissecting them to the point of joyless mechanics. And you know what else? That formal debrief may not be as effective. Indeed, there's something about celebration—taking the time to shine your light on the positive stuff of life, play, and have some fun—that can make people more creative.

You aren't maximizing your learning and growth potential without incorporating play. Yep. You heard it here! Get out the volleyball, art supplies, and improv games! The fantastic book *Play: How It Shapes the Brain, Opens the Imagination, and Invigorates the Soul* by Dr. Stuart Brown, MD, underscores this, discussing how play can help contribute to better brainstorming sessions and more. "Parents and educators, corporate leaders, and others need to become convinced by the evidence that long-term life skills and a rewarding sense of fulfillment—and yes, performance—are more the by-product of play-related activities than forced performance," asserts Dr. Brown.[10]

Playing might translate into learning more from your victories in innovative, useful ways. That's right. That celebratory outing, in which you welcome in play, may be what you need to win the next big client! So it's time to start saying, "Let's have fun with this." And following through.

How can you use enjoyable activities to acquire information and insights about your achievements? Here's one way: I created an entertaining, play-promoting strategy called the Victory Awards. It allows you to concurrently celebrate and learn from your victory by inventing fun, perhaps mildly absurd awards. These creative, positively focused prizes will enable you to enjoy reflecting on your success, as well as provide specific details and clarity about what assisted you in accomplishing your goal. Here are some sample awards to create:

- **You Kept Me Running Award:** What thought, mantra, or motto helped you persevere—especially when you really wanted to give up?

- **Awesome Assistance Award:** Which website, video, podcast, book, or other resource deserves a sincere, "I couldn't have done it without you"?
- **Best Breakthrough Moment:** What pivotal instance, experience, or realization brought it all together, provided clear direction, and accelerated your progress to the finish line?
- **Best Soundtrack Award:** What songs, albums, or musicians helped you focus and do the work that led to your success? This could be an actual song or playlist, a genre of music, the sound of the birds outside, or silence. It could even be a thank-you to noise-canceling headphones!
- **Best in Show Snacks:** An award to honor the food that fueled you, that was decently healthy, and that you actually remembered to eat.
- **The Ugly Beast Award:** Yep, an award to acknowledge what really *didn't* assist you on your journey. Examples of this may be: negative self-talk ("I can't do this! Why did I even start this?"), chronically staying up late, not eating breakfast, or forgetting to make copies of your presentation. It might be when you started comparing yourself with someone else, or felt discouraged, anxious, or not good enough, and you almost gave up, believing you'd never achieve your goal. Now that you've identified this unhelpful, ugly beast, you can watch for it. It won't stand a chance against you and your celebrations next time!
- **Friend 'Til the End Award:** This prize thanks the faithful friend who was there with you from the beginning and made your trek a little easier: an encouraging colleague, buddy, family member, pet, or even trusty computer; an inspiring quote you kept on your wall; your favorite tea or coffee pick-me-up that was always there when ya needed it.

- **What I Wish I'd Known Before I Started All This Award:** If you could time-travel back to right before you began the adventure that led to this victory, what would you tell your pre-victory self that might have made it easier as you worked toward this win?

TAKE ACTION

Now you try! What are some recent victories you've experienced in your life? Think about major goals you've accomplished or small but necessary stepping-stone advances you've made toward turning your dreams into realities. What insights can you garner from reflecting on these successes? How might thinking about past processes help you prosper in current or future endeavors?

Choose one of the wins you identified and create at least two related Victory Awards. Use the award titles I offered or generate new ones you feel are goofy, applicable, and/or useful. Give yourself time to play! After creating the awards, focus on what you learned, anything that surprised you, and concrete ways you might use this information on your next major mountain climb.

In the meantime, I'd personally like to present this exercise with the Terrific Take Action Award for assisting you with identifying what contributed to your triumph! Bravo!

You can create Victory Awards after any achievement to help you recognize what aided your win. Additionally, in professional or educational settings, this can serve as a celebratory, team-building exercise.

See? Fun can move people forward!

3. Get Refueled

Phew! After all that fun, who needs a rest? *Rest? Dr. A! You've got to be kidding!* I'm not talking about nap time—unless that helps you. I'm simply reminding you that, again, you can use your celebration as recovery time! As we discussed, even the most elite athletes—some of the hardest-working folks out there—pause to refuel between competitions. That's why it's called the *off*-season. And you need to pause, too—even if it's only for a few hours. Just like your muscles need to recover between workouts to optimize your athleticism, your brain needs that pause to recalibrate, energize, and give you the edge you need for high performance. Giving equal weight to your recovery—knowing when to pump the brakes and rejoice in your win—is what keeps you from burning out. You just exerted tremendous energy to accomplish this current victory. This short celebration gives you time to prepare for your next project, goal, race, or dream.

Refueling does *not* mean you are being lazy. In fact, it's a form of preparation. I get it: Spectacular views assuredly await you atop wondrous mountains in the distance, as well. But that doesn't mean you can't stop, eat a granola bar, sit down or stretch your legs for a moment, snap a celebratory selfie, and breathe in the air on this *current* mountaintop first. As Nelson Mandela said: "Remember to celebrate milestones as you prepare for the road ahead."

Here's a great example: Have you ever completed a big project or deadline, exhaled, and then finally stopped to look around, only to realize that your home is a hot mess? This is an understandable development. You've simply been so busy focusing on one time-sensitive project that you let other things go—laundry, bills, grocery shopping. Giving yourself permission to pause—to celebrate by gifting yourself a few days to get your life in order and reassess where you're at with fundamental self-care—allows you to be at your best and ready as the next project begins. You can ask yourself: Did anything slip or go unaddressed while you were striving to achieve this victory? Have you been getting at least seven hours of sleep every night? Have you been making the time to exercise and expend some of the anxious energy that can accompany toiling toward an important goal?

This is part of refueling and setting yourself up for success.

Among the most common issues that come up in my office, as my patients sit across from me, frayed, anxious, and stressed to the brim, is the idea of both moving goalposts and constantly moving on to the next. These concepts are related but different. When high achievers continually move goalposts, reestablishing new metrics for what victory would mean, they effectively make it impossible to cross the finish line. They, for instance, land an important new teaching job and, before even feeling proud, move the goalpost of success to mean being a tenured professor. There's no chance to celebrate a win because, arguably, there is no win. There's only a new definition of success to work toward. High achievers seeking perfection do this because they are perpetually trying to prove their worth.

When high achievers constantly move on to the next, they give themselves a chance to meet their goals. But they move so quickly on to the next project that they never give themselves a beat to feel excited and grateful, bask in congratulations, or pause to remember the feeling of arrival. That victory is too quickly forgotten, so they don't reap the benefits of achievement. I see it happen time and time again: A client comes in after a critical stakeholders' meeting that they'd been stressing hard about and that actually went well. They've moved so quickly on to the next stressor or important presentation that they don't even remember being anxious about this past one. And they don't recognize how important it is to pause and appreciate the victory. Don't let Post-Participation Amnesia—which we discussed in Essential #3—rob you of the important opportunity to celebrate because you're afraid something new won't go well! Empower yourself to store the positive memory.

Moving on to the next can also be a result of external factors. There are company cultures that glorify a relentless pace and unrealistic workload, which would discourage you from taking a pause. The nature of your job may also make it difficult to celebrate if you have overlapping projects or deadlines, like lawyers who are working on multiple cases at once or writers who have several articles due at a time.

As a result, it's up to you to make the time to celebrate. This might feel hard because constantly stepping on the gas pedal is so ingrained that you might not think to pump the brakes sometimes. (Don't make me extend the obvious car metaphors!) Remember: A pause is not paralysis. It's proactive! And that pause to refuel has to be intentional and self-motivated or it may not happen, which is why cultivating a habit of celebrating at the completion of each goal is so helpful.

Otherwise what I hear is, "Sorry, Dr. A, no time. I'll stop to celebrate when... I'll feel less anxious when... I know I'll plan in that day off or special vacation right after I finish..." But often those very same clients have expressed similar sentiments right before embarking upon the projects ending in *these* current victories, as well. It's a vicious cycle. And if you don't stop to refuel after this current victory, what's to say you will make time after the next win or the one after that—if burnout doesn't set in first? That's why the refueling must start now!

> **Pro Tip:** Take your pause outside and in nature instead of at your desk. No need to run or even stroll. Robust research shows that just being in a green space has quantifiable benefits, linked to "improved attention, lower stress, better mood, reduced risk of psychiatric disorders and even upticks in empathy and cooperation."[11] So just sit yourself on a bench, pause to celebrate, and let the goodness soak in.

4. Connect with Others

You don't have to refuel alone! In fact, celebrating victories connects people in multiple ways. And as we know, healthy relationships (aka connections) are essential to sustained success. This is, of course, most evident when a goal is shared. Going out after work with a team of colleagues to mark a collective win creates a fantastic foundation for bonding. Everyone is feeling good! Each person has contributed to creating forward momentum. If you're a team member, you might help organize an after-work trivia night, snacks, or a softball game in the park to mark a met goal. If you're in a senior leadership position, you can set an example by scheduling team-building outings immediately after important milestones to celebrate a team's accomplishments and unify your employees. Bowling, anyone? When people feel their work is appreciated, they're more likely to collaborate and come to work each day with high morale. And that helps teams move forward together.

The success provides a common, positive point of attention for you and the people around you. You gather together with the shared purpose of actively applauding something positive. It disrupts the daily routine with an enjoyable, meaningful moment and collectively refocuses everyone's flashlights on what's good.

And this is even true when the achievement appears to be yours alone and applauded by others. It's why no one stands at the podium under glistening lights after winning an Academy Award, for example, and says, "Thanks! I did this all myself!" They thank everyone who supported them along the way, which both moves us as an audience and invests us in their continued success. The show of gratitude makes us root for them! And sometimes even spurs conversations about who we'd thank if it was our moment.

So, your personal win can also become a reminder to pause and appreciate other people's contributions to your life along the way—like the teacher who inspired you by supporting your writing all those years ago, the devoted parent who hauled you from soccer game to soccer game for decades, the encouraging coach who believed in you even as you struggled, the boss who offered schedule flexibility when he knew times were tough, even the patient friend or tech expert who talked you through your computer crisis!

Throwing yourself a party or even just asking friends to hang out and toast your win might seem self-centered. But when you mark your successes by including and honoring others, you are actively choosing to make time for social connection, say thank you, *and* celebrate the victories. Yep, three birds with one stone. You're living the messages of Essentials #4, #6, and #7 all at the same time. That's excellence. And it can provide a mega energy boost for you and all of those included.

If you're struggling to notice when to celebrate your own victories, you can start by celebrating other people's wins. Yes, sharing in joy and festivity with friends, family members, colleagues, and classmates after they succeed in their endeavors can actually improve your relationships with them and often enhance your mood and motivation, as well. People will notice if you stand with them through all the seasons of life, good and bad, as both an empathetic ear and an enthusiastic fan. So when you see that someone else was able to persevere and achieve their dreams, let it inspire you. I was so proud of my patient Emma, who was struggling to finish her dissertation. She said that attending a party for her classmate who had just successfully defended his own dissertation gave her the final push she needed. Instead of spiraling into self-defeating self-talk and comparison—What's wrong with me? I should have already completed my dissertation, too—she found a way to benefit from rejoicing in his triumph, realizing that there was enough success to go around. Using positive self-talk, she got excited for them both! As author Louise Hay famously said: "I rejoice in the success of others, knowing that there is plenty for us all."

A few months later, when Emma finished her own dissertation, she celebrated that gleefully, too.

TAKE ACTION

We looked at and cultivated gratitude for the people who were there for you in the swamps. Now let's grab the confetti and spotlight who sat by your side for the victories. Who helped you achieve goals along the way? Are there people you haven't yet thanked for their support? Let celebration create connection for you! This week, take the time to thank at least one person who assisted you in a victory, be it small or large. Tell them how they helped you succeed and why it was so meaningful to you.

Bonus Boost: Did anyone in your life recently meet a big goal? Did you celebrate them? This week, celebrate someone else's win. Treat the person to coffee or a mani-pedi, give a card saying, "Congrats!" or offer to take them out to celebrate. Connecting with others by celebrating the victories is a win for everyone!

5. Create Reminders

Remember back in the day when you were a kid and used to have an award ceremony after every achievement? The end of the school year alone was a cluster of recitals, graduation ceremonies, and field days, leaving you with a slew of awards, diplomas, medals, and congratulatory ice cream cones and parties. No doubt, you have happy memories of—and cherished keepsakes from—those times. These recollections of celebration are more than just "nice." They're the meaningful stuff of life and also powerful, formative reminders of what's possible. Looking back on those celebrations can activate your memories of previous successes and help you. They remind you that you are capable of achieving your goals—you've dreamed big dreams, put in the work, and reaped the rewards. And you'll do it again.

Taking time to recognize victories allows you to create concrete reminders for yourself. And you know when those reminders come in handy? In the swamps. When you are at mile twenty in your marathon.

Just days away from your important exam or presentation. Or halfway through your internship, manuscript, or major project and ask yourself: What was I thinking trying to do this?! When you start to feel the nauseous, jittery, visceral feelings of anxiety begin. And when pernicious, self-defeating self-talk starts stirring up worry, self-doubt, and panic. Break out the trophies! Bring on the memories!

When you notice these unhelpful thoughts and feelings beginning to creep in, look at pictures of past celebrations, review the Victory Awards you created after your last success, or take time to stand in front of your diploma or other tangible symbols (medals, certificates, memorabilia, and so on) of your hard work leading to successful completion. This will help remind you: You are awesome. Then you can think about all the past trials you've endured and bested. Finally, remember: The secret to courageously achieving your goals is to keep going. Just keep moving forward. You've done it before. And you have the memories to prove it. You'll do it again.

TAKE ACTION

What will be *your* concrete reminders? A special memento or photo on your desk from a post-win celebration, an award or certificate on your wall? A small keepsake? Something you buy for yourself, are gifted, or discover outside—a beautiful shell or rock—to remind you of an important day? An inspirational quote or meaningful words that capture the spirit of your triumph, or a souvenir commemorating your success?

Here's an easy way to create a reminder: First, identify a victory. Ask yourself: What did I do? What did that feel like? Why was it meaningful to me? Just as we did with Maui, visualize the celebration of your success. When I found out I had secured a book deal, for example, I felt elated, exhilarated, and joyful in a way I can rarely remember feeling in my life. I had wanted to be an author since I was a small child! To celebrate, I blasted the 10,000 Maniacs song "These Are Days" in my living room and danced by myself with total abandon! My acknowledgment of the moment extended all the way through the entire song. In this way, I installed those positive feelings, that special memory. Now every time I hear that song, I feel a wave of happiness and gratitude.

Picture yourself in the moment after a major triumph—tap into all of your senses. Then, once you've found that inspiring mindset, pull out a Post-it and jot down your victory moment to stick to your bulletin board, desk, or wall. It can even be in a kind of code so that only you understand if you want to keep it private. For instance, mine might just say, "10,000" or "These Are Days" or even the date it happened. But each time you look at it, you'll be reminded of your ability, of how much you have the potential to achieve. It's not too late to snap the picture in your mind to celebrate the win! Just like going to Maui in our minds, we can go to this awesome moment and use it as encouragement and fuel.

YOU DESERVE TO ENJOY!

Why do we do the work? Why do we achieve? As we've discussed, if our motivation is gaining approval from others, our path is destined to be rife with disappointment. Conversely, what if the whole point of doing the work, putting in all of that time and energy and care, is to have these moments? If you're not enjoying your success, then what are you doing all this for?

Enjoying your life doesn't make you lazy. It's not going to put you behind or set you back, whatever that might mean to you. So instead of trying to prove to the world how lovable you are, show yourself the love! Celebrate you. Celebrate the people who have helped you. Let yourself cultivate a sense of joy!

Just as it's important to decrease your anxiety, it's essential to increase your joy in order to be happy and high-achieving.

"If all you are doing is just going from task to task without feeling—then all you are doing is working like a robot," write Benjamin

Cheyette, MD, and Sarah Cheyette, MD, in *Psychology Today*. "The celebration of achievement and the positive emotion you feel is what tells your brain: 'This is why it was worth it to put in all that hard work.'"[12] So grant yourself the time to enjoy it. After all, enjoying one win will set you up to enjoy more! In the wise words of Madonna, "Come on! Let's celebrate!"

TOP TAKEAWAYS

- Fight that negativity bias! Pause to celebrate and intentionally install positive experiences in your mind!
- Use your memories of past successes as fuel while you climb your next mountain.
- Fun can move you forward.
- "We don't just celebrate the win; we celebrate *to* win."[13]
- Create concrete reminders of your victories to help you remember what you are capable of and to bolster you during tough moments.
- Celebration creates connection!

ESSENTIAL #8

CURATE MEANINGFUL GOALS, CREATE YOUR LEGACY— START NOW!

What you leave behind is not what is engraved in stone monuments, but what is woven into the lives of others.

—Pericles

We've talked about how to set specific, doable goals that we want to work on. Goals that empower us to say, "I can do this." We've discussed the importance of celebrating, pausing to rejoice at the summit of the mountain, in order to benefit from our successes. In this last essential, we're learning to level up in the ultimate way: curating our goals to create the meaningful lives and legacies we want for ourselves.

Meaningful? I know. That may not seem like a simple ask. After all, prompted by All-or-Nothing Thinking, by the erroneous idea that there's only one correct way to succeed based on societal standards, anxious high achievers are inclined to say things like, "I want to make sure I'm doing life *right*." That suggests a narrow metric for success. And who decides what "right" means, anyway? Is it your parents? A younger—and possibly outdated—version of yourself? A series of influences impressed upon you as you ride the conveyer belt? It's very important—dare I say *essential*—to figure out who is defining success for you and, therefore, informing your aspirations.

In many ways, being guided by meaning is another way of saying that we need to build our choices and our lives around what we—and not others—truly want and value. That way we'll make choices with intention, ensuring that we're not riding a conveyer belt of someone else's choosing. It's how we control the narrative and create the future we envision. Meaning empowers us to choose what we want, believe in ourselves, and focus on meetable goals.

When you identify and work toward goals that are authentically important to *you* (not just acquiescing to what others expect of you), you are much less likely to quit—and much more likely to enjoy your life. Perhaps sage Austrian psychiatrist and Holocaust survivor Viktor Frankl said it best: "What man actually needs is not a tensionless state but rather the striving and struggling for a worthwhile goal, a freely chosen task."[1] Indeed, it is not the elimination of all anxiety that will help you feel happier, but rather ensuring you have a meaningful goal or goals to work toward, channeling your energy into creating or contributing to something bigger. And when you take the focus off having to prove yourself—how smart you sound, what you look like, what other people think about you—and instead focus your energy and attention on working toward a purposeful aim of your own choosing, that's when you'll thrive.

You need to work toward accomplishments that actually matter to you so you are proud of your life and legacy and how you spend your time and energy. And you're going to need to trust yourself to choose what you want, to choose meaningful goals based on what you value. That's what will set you up to be both happy and high-achieving.

WHAT WILL *YOUR* LEGACY BE?

I know. "Legacy" is a word with grandiose implications. It brings to mind historical figures like Harriet Tubman, Mother Teresa, Mahatma Gandhi, Anne Frank, Albert Einstein, Nelson Mandela, Andrew Carnegie, and Oprah Winfrey—and so many more portraits of excellence we look to for inspiration.

So your first thought might be: What do those people have to do with me?

Actually, this concept isn't just for history's greatest icons. You, too, can create a legacy—simply by being mindful about how you set your goals.

I often tell my clients, "Life is about choices. Choose wisely!" Each meaningful goal that you set and accomplish is one individual step toward your larger contribution. Legacy is the culmination of those goals, what you want to contribute to the world. It's the greater purpose that motivates and moves you forward.

This isn't about impressive obituaries and eulogies, though it's easy for high achievers to fall into that trap. Nope. Those are about approval from others, again. This is literally about asking yourself: What would *you* feel proud of? What are your goals and dreams? It's about answering that fundamental question: What is meaningful, on a large scale, to you? What do you really, *really* want?

When people think about their legacy, it's often in the context of one big win. And from the outside, that often feels true. When a beloved writer comes out with her new Pulitzer Prize–worthy book, it may seem like some overnight achievement. But think of how many early mornings and revisions and frustrated roadblocks had to be traversed for every great American novel. Think of the myriad incarnations of your favorite song that existed before it was considered ready for the airwaves. These goals—and the legacy they're implicit in building—are all the more meaningful because of the hard work behind them. These big wins are made up of a million small achievements (which we're going to remember to celebrate, right?) that make up a larger legacy. Sometimes what's most meaningful is not even the book or song or app or advertisement or whatever it is that you've contributed to putting out into the world, but rather the way those creations and contributions, small and large, have impacted a single soul.

When we think about an incredibly prolific writer like Ray Bradbury, for example, is his legacy built on one great book or on the collection of all his books and the way they've delighted and edified readers? Some might argue that his greatest contribution is *Zen in the Art of Writing* rather than his many novels, as it helped other writers in their quest for their own meaningful goals. And he would never have been able to write that had it not been for the foundation he created with his many fiction books. This is what we mean by determining what makes us feel personally proud or fulfilled. This is what we mean by legacy.

So when we think about legacy, what we're really talking about is achieving a string of meaningful goals over time—big and small. That's why it's so important you don't burn yourself out. You need to invest in your energy—fuel yourself with sleep, healthy nutrition, hydration, nature, exercise, relaxation, and time for friends and fun—so you can endure, persevere, and live a long life filled with legacy-creating moments.

What will be *your* legacy? Conducting research that advances science or your chosen field? Caring for ill patients or animals at a hospital? Upholding justice in a courtroom? Adding beauty into the world with your art or food or creative projects? Innovating new ways to improve people's lives? Working to protect the environment for future generations? Ensuring you treat all employees with respect? Helping others by lending a hand at your local library or nonprofit organization? Raising children to be kind citizens of the world? These are just a few examples of meaning-based goals that could help you enjoy excellence in your lifetime.

Moreover, when you work toward freely chosen aims that you are deeply motivated to achieve, you will remain determined to keep moving forward—despite the inevitable swamps of life. 'Cause we know the swamps will come. But our sense of purpose can keep us on track, regardless of setbacks and frustrations. The world needs our unique gifts. As Nobel Prize–winning scientist Marie Curie once said, "We must have perseverance and above all confidence in ourselves. We must believe that we are gifted for something and that this thing must be attained." We need to choose a purposeful goal and then trust ourselves to attain it.

REVISITING YOUR VISION BOARD...NOW

As high achievers, we're prone to focus on the outcome, but the question of legacy isn't about the result of any one achievement itself. It's about what you want to experience and leave behind. In your life, what do you want to have done that matters to you? Leaving a legacy you're proud of depends on mindfully choosing how you spend your time and energy.

For example, I'm Scottish—my father's father emigrated from Dundee in the late 1920s—and I've never been to Scotland. I really want to go there, and I am now finally planning a trip. It's important to me—because it's about honoring my value of family, as well as exploring my own identity. It's about being able to have adventures in my life beyond the status quo and paying tribute to my true interests.

Building your vision board, or curating your goals and dreams for your life, is not about impressing people. It's about ensuring you live based on your values.

As a strategy for determining meaningful goals, I often ask my patients to list their top five values. This is much harder than you might imagine. And that's usually because people haven't thought about their life in those terms before. But consider how much that information might help inform your decisions and goal setting moving forward. So it's beneficial to really think about: What do you care most about? About family? About knowledge? About growth? About health? About kindness? About joy? About friendship? About wealth?

About humor? About courage? About love? About integrity? About stability? About service? About peace? About respect? About fun? About adventure? About changing the world for the better? Understanding your own values helps you work toward creating the legacy of your dreams... now.

THIS IS YOUR MOMENT!

As Buddhist monk and peace activist Thich Nhat Hanh said, "The best way to take care of the future is to take care of the present moment." That's a strong argument for self-care but also for actively working toward goals in the present moment that you feel proud of. That's how you create your legacy. It's not about saying you'll do it tomorrow. Use today to proactively build meaning into your life's work. Basically, *now* is the best time to think about what you want to devote your time, energy, and life toward achieving and experiencing. Why? Because now is what we have. Don't wait until you're diagnosed with a major illness or until the end of your life to do something meaningful. Start now! Literally, the phrase I hear most often at final sessions with my patients is, "I wish I had started this sooner, Dr. A." My clients mean that they wish they had started sooner to find balance in their lives, to feel better. But they'd put off making time for themselves because they believed that waylaying their self-care was a necessary sacrifice for success. That's why starting now is so important. You deserve to feel your best, to *be* your best, today.

So, this is your time to think about: What do you really want for yourself? What indelible mark do you want to leave on the world that only you can, in a way that feels doable? That honors you. Not for the sake of sounding cool or one-upping others. And most important, why? A powerful "why" is what will keep you going and dedicated to working diligently to accomplish your goals on even the hardest of days.

What *do* you want your legacy to be? What *is* on your vision board? This isn't about morality or spirituality (unless it is for you). It's about figuring out what matters to you at your core, often within the Three Pillars of home, health, and work. This can mean many different things to different people: You may want to consider your dreams for your career and professional development, relationships, family, activities, travel, and so on. Maybe you simply want to live by the ocean.

I encourage you to write a list or, if you're crafty, create a vision board that reflects what you most want for your life. Really take some time and let yourself generate as many ideas as you want on this one.

TAKE ACTION

It can be challenging to determine your top values in order to guide your meaningful goals and, ultimately, your legacy. Begin by asking yourself:

- Who are your heroes? Who do you look up to?
- What attributes do they have that you most admire? What seemed to be most important to them?
- What do you want to emulate?

Additionally, ask yourself: If you have extra fun money to spend, how do you spend it? Where do you spend your time? I spend money on books because I value continuous learning. Some people spend time and money visiting art museums because beauty is important to them. This can be a window into your values and a quick hack for determining if your priorities and actions are aligned. If your answer is, "Mostly I'm just at work. I spend money on takeout. I don't even value what I'm doing"—there's your red flag! Maybe you're not making time for the things you *do* value. I have a lot of lawyer clients, for example, who love being creative but don't make time to honor that for themselves. Make sure you're making space for what you care about most.

BACK TO THE FUTURE

Your past choices don't necessarily have to define your legacy. We've all heard of the Nobel Prize, but do you know what the founder of the Nobel Prize invented? Honestly, I didn't until recently reading a *Harvard Business Review* article. And perhaps that's exactly what Alfred Nobel was hoping.

The *HBR* story "How to Think About Building Your Legacy" recounts the life of Alfred Nobel.[2] In 1888, when Alfred's brother passed away, a newspaper editor mistakenly wrote the obituary as if Alfred himself had died. Alfred, of course, read it—and it was not favorable. Because he was the inventor of dynamite (yep—explosives!), the writer referred to him as "the merchant of death." People now speculate that this crossroads likely motivated Alfred, who was an extremely wealthy man, to decide to bequeath his fortune to the creation of five prizes honoring excellence in medicine, literature, physics, chemistry, and peace.[3] These renowned Nobel Prizes have thus been awarded since 1901, with economic sciences added as the sixth prize category in 1968.[4]

So now we revere the name "Nobel" rather than revile it.

Nothing like being reminded of your mortality—and legacy!—to help you get clear about how you want to be remembered.

Here's where it gets interesting for you: I want you to imagine that you just traveled forward into the future. You're now eighty years old. You were rummaging around in the attic and came across your old vision board. How do you feel about your list from the perspective of your older self? If you achieved and experienced everything on it, are you proud of what your life consisted of and represented? Is there an item that feels particularly meaningful or most exciting? Do you feel anything is missing that you'd want to add?

Ask yourself:

- What do you want to be able to say you achieved in your life? How you grew as a person, or what you gained, shared, completed, learned, or experienced?

- What do you want to be able to say you contributed to your community, environment, or the world to help make it better?
- How do you want to be remembered by future generations?

Reflecting on questions like these will help you clearly ascertain which aspects of life you most value and which experiences are most meaningful to you. That clarity, in turn, will inform what long-term goals you want to set, how you prioritize short-term goals, and how you'll want to strategically choose to focus your time, attention, and energy on each day.

Important to note: Your list will change over time—with additions and subtractions—and some constants will remain. Take special note of the "why" behind the ones that linger. It can illuminate what's most important to you. But it's totally normal and healthy to let your desires evolve and transform over time. What you would select for your vision board at eighteen years old would almost assuredly differ from what you'd choose at age twenty-eight, thirty-eight, forty-eight, and beyond. That's why it's especially beneficial to build in pauses (perhaps during periods of celebrating victories) to revisit and reassess your list of meaningful life goals.

Of course, envisioning your legacy is one thing. Taking action on it is another. It's not enough to create a vision board. You've also got to do the work.

EVERYDAY PROGRESS

Moving forward doesn't mean you'll set and complete all of your meaningful goals today. Slow your roll, my high-achieving friend! Moving forward just means making progress. Remember what Thich Nhat Hanh said? We're going to focus on the present as a portal to success in the future.

As we know, progress, not perfection, creates an excellent life. One with a whole lot less stress and anxiety and much more meaning and joy.

So identify your meaningful and doable goals toward your eventual legacy and then prioritize doing the work to make progress on them—every day. Yep. Every. Single. Day. Do something that honors your greatest aims on the regular. Even something super small. This will ensure that you keep moving toward joy, ease, and success instead of staying stuck.

In addition to completing specific, doable weekly goals, recognize that your micro-wins will help you move forward. Your in-the-moment choices. The seemingly inconsequential "drop in the bucket" present-moment progress that will actually lead you to full-bucket future success.

I'm talking about those stolen moments where you turn on that app or pull out flash cards on the subway in service of learning that language you've always wanted to speak, or walk the long way so you can listen to music and notice the scenery. I mean leaving your phone in the other room while you spend quality time with your romantic partner. This is remembering to set your alarm for 10:00 p.m. so you can get to bed early and get restful sleep. Yes, even saying "I got this" to yourself before an interview or exam instead of focusing on all that might go wrong. This is all in service of meeting your smaller meaningful goals so you can build them up to a giant legacy. Progress!

It means, if you want to be a writer, write. Every day. Even if that's just scrawling a few lines on the back of a napkin or in your Notes app during lunch. If you want to be more grateful, list five things for which you're grateful right now and then keep doing that each day to remind yourself to focus on the good. If you dream of a new career, sign up for a course or a class to work toward that, or schedule a meetup with someone who is already doing what you want to do. Try to learn a little bit more every day.

Don't let daily inaction or perfection-seeking paralysis create inertia. Do not slip into that high-achiever avoidance pitfall! Build momentum with everyday progress to create the life you really want for yourself—one with purpose. You can choose continual growth over stagnation. Progress over perfection. Meaning over empty toiling. Every day.

TAKE ACTION

Legacy is about feeling deep satisfaction with how you spend your time on earth. It inspires you to work to meet your meaningful goals. Feeling pleased and at peace with yourself is a game-changer! So do one thing today that makes you feel proud. That prioritizes your highest values.

Think small but purposeful. Pick up a piece of litter and help protect the environment. Reach out to a friend, family member, or neighbor who you think might be lonely or struggling. Invest in your health—go for a walk outside or choose to eat fresh green vegetables—to energize yourself and fuel your body and brain for optimal long-term functioning. Say a genuine thank-you to someone. Connect with a person in your community with a smile or by offering a simple, "It's great to see you." And give yourself credit for doing your best to create your unique legacy—starting now.

KEEP PLUGGING ALONG

You're moving forward. That's great news! After all, as we know, approach—as opposed to avoidance—is the ultimate remedy for anxiety. Now, keep going. Time for some expectation management. You probably already know this. But it's easy to forget, especially when you're striving for excellence and then an unexpected swamp—or what feels like an endless slew of swamps—appears to suck you in. Things of greatness take time and hard work and rarely have a linear path. We must acknowledge life's circuitous nature, the fact that elements outside your control exist throughout the journey to your goals and dreams. Even the goals with meaning behind them. "Let me tell you the secret that has led me to my goal," French scientist Louis Pasteur once said. "My strength lies solely in my tenacity."

Like all excellent people, Pasteur endured setbacks and yet he persisted. And his contributions helped change the world for the better!

Yours will, too.

Like Pasteur, you will need to accept mistakes as part of the process. You will face obstacles, stumbles, and slips en route to achieving your meaningful goals. But reminding yourself of the inherent purpose, the meaning itself, will help pull you through toward your legacy.

THE POWER OF TRUST: THE DOTS WILL CONNECT

Now for the "secret sauce"—the final ingredient that clinches the recipe for your long-term happiness and meaningful success. The pièce de résistance of your legacy soufflé. "You can't connect the dots looking forward; you can only connect them looking backwards," said Steve Jobs in his Stanford University commencement speech. "So you have to trust that the dots will somehow connect in your future. You have to trust in something—your gut, destiny, life, karma, whatever. This approach has never let me down, and it has made all the difference in my life."[5]

Trust. It truly is the key ingredient to being a happy high achiever. Without trust, or what is tantamount to the belief we've discussed before, even the meaningful goals can't come to fruition. You must believe in your capacity for an excellent life in order to feel fueled. You have to trust that you're capable. And your goals must reflect that. When you choose trust over fear, it energizes you and keeps you moving forward. Fear will try to deceive you into believing that things won't ever work out and that the dots won't ever connect. And yet somehow, they do.

REJECTING FEAR, ACCEPTING SHIFTS

But sometimes, things look different than expected when they work out. There's a risk of attaching to one objective so intensely that you're unable to release and pivot in service of your purpose. Often the way to hold on to your belief and trust can be rooted in your *why*. That allows you to be less fixated on a single outcome. Most of the time, if there is something you really, really want, you can and will find a way. But you may need to let go of or quit the original version of the goal. And that's okay. Your ultimate success might not look as you initially imagined, but if you can detach from the very specific idea of what you envisioned, you can make it happen. That way you can choose meaningful goals that are within your control and trust in your ability to achieve them, knowing that they might evolve and change. For example, with this project, I set out to be an author. Notice my goal was not "I want to be a bestselling author," because I'm not in direct control of that. Once you've set a goal, then you can ask yourself what it is about that objective that motivates you: Is it a desire to help people? Prestige? Financial security? Giving yourself a platform or voice? Once you know your *why*, it's possible to determine other goals that might meet that same need if the first path doesn't work. And you can trust that, when you use that *why* as your guide, you'll be able to find opportunities that offer the core element you desire.

Fear about whether things will work out in the future is one thing: distraction. And it causes you to lose your focus. It will mire you in worry. And as you know, worry will zap your energy. Fear will hijack your attention and make it impossible to invest your full focus on accomplishing your meaningful goals.

Your present-moment focus, where you choose to aim your energy and attention right now, is your power. So retrain your flashlight on what serves your long-term success—what you're doing right *now*. Don't get distracted by the future!

Remember that Vonnegut quote from Essential #4: "The secret to success in every human endeavor is total concentration."[6] You know how you cultivate total concentration? Trust.

Let me explain: Trust or belief that you can do something is crucial so that you can focus on the *how* instead of being distracted by the question of whether you *can*. You simply cannot fully concentrate without trust. Many of my high-achieving patients question, "Am I cut out for this?" They don't trust in their ability and it amplifies their anxiety, causing them to lose focus. What they would ideally be asking instead is, "Do I like doing this? Is it meaningful to me? Does it reflect my values?"

Trust will allow you to focus on what you are doing. It will allow you to fully engage. You will be empowered to set meaningful, legacy-creating goals and then invest in the process. You'll persevere—even when, *especially* when, you are uncertain about how the dots are all going to ultimately connect. Trust will free up your energy and liberate your attention so you can put your time and effort toward finding lasting fulfillment.

After all, the opposite of trust is doubt. And it floods you with that pesky fear and worry. It pushes you to try to control what isn't within your control and limit yourself, wary of any risk because you worry, "What if it doesn't work out?" Doubt splits your attention and depletes your energy. You may set the deepest, most meaningful goals, but your doubt will keep you in an endless, time-wasting, energy-zapping loop of worrying about the future. So choose trust!

BELIEVE IN SOMETHING

Similar to Steve Jobs, I've found from working with my patients that it doesn't matter what their particular belief system is; they just need to trust in something. Some patients trust the Universe, God, or the Divine, where others source trust in nature, reason, or the laws of physics. I encourage you to use whatever works for you. I've absolutely found that trusting in something bigger is incredibly helpful for people. First, it can empower you to let go of trying to control or micromanage every step of your journey, which you won't be able to do anyway. If you attempt it, the rigidity will only significantly drain your energy and negatively impact your mood and relationships. Second, belief can be a source of strength and comfort as you traverse challenging swamps. It helps remind you: You are not alone. There are larger constants in life that you can lean on.

NOW IS THE TIME TO TRUST YOURSELF

Equally important is trusting yourself. As we've discussed, you have to believe in your capacity to make progress and honor your values, first and foremost. That doesn't mean you can magically do it all yourself or that you can achieve meaningful goals without doing the work. And some degree of self-doubt is understandable. But we can combat that with tools we've learned throughout the essentials. Return to the memories you installed with celebrations to remind yourself of what you've been able to accomplish in the past, even against the odds. Remember all the swamps you've traversed and survived, bolstered by newfound understanding, knowledge, and strengths. Draw on your earned courage! Surround yourself with people who lift you up. Remind yourself of your higher purpose. Instead of focusing on how far you need to go, concentrate on how far you've come. You've been able to pull out even unlikely successes in the past. Trust yourself to do it again now.

Previously, we navigated uncertainty with curiosity. Now we navigate it with trust and belief, as well. Remember "Come what may"? It's the phrase we use to reinforce our belief in ourselves! Trust yourself: Come what may, you will figure out, with assistance as needed, how to keep moving forward. And trusting fuels you with the courage to take action and fortifies you with the confidence that your efforts (no matter where they lead) are *meaningful*.

Ultimately, choosing trust will let you stay tenacious and even hopeful. It keeps your flashlight focused where it needs to be.

Life is worth the work to do meaningful things, to dream big. So set your purposeful goals. Then buckle up and do the work. And just keep moving forward. Your lasting legacy starts now!

TOP TAKEAWAYS

- Life is about choices. Choose wisely!
- Strategically manage your expectations. Greatness takes time and hard work and rarely has a linear path—stay tenacious!
- Now is the best time to think about what you want to devote your time, energy, and life to in order to build a legacy you value. Because now is what we have.
- Progress, not perfection, creates an excellent life.
- Trust the dots to connect—and trust yourself to keep moving forward toward achieving your meaningful goals.

PART THREE

KEEP MOVING FORWARD

ENJOYING A LIFETIME OF EXCELLENCE

Yesterday is gone. Tomorrow has not yet come.
We have only today. Let us begin.

—Mother Teresa

These 8 Essentials are meant to support you throughout your life—as you navigate swamps, climb mountains, celebrate at the summits, and keep moving forward. They're not just one and done.

The great news is that, as you've worked your way through this book, you've collected a multitude of tools along the way—for overcoming anxiety, managing stress, and energizing yourself for success.

Well, pack some trail mix, because the journey continues. It's going to take some effort to live sustainably as a happy high achiever, to maintain the progress you've made and continue crushing it and reveling in it at the same time.

So how can you consistently implement these principles and their related strategies into your daily routine, keeping your self-doubt and worry at bay and paving the way for a lifetime of excellence?

You can:

- Do the Work
- Be Kind to Yourself While You Do the Work
- Love the Work... 'Cause the Work Is Your Life!

DO THE WORK

You're a high achiever. You're used to putting in work. So, what does that mean here?

Well, first it means redefining your end goal. I know it's confusing because the word "happy" is key to where we're hoping to land. We want to be happy high achievers, of course! But as we've learned throughout this process, happiness comes from optimizing thoughts and behaviors. So that's our real aim. With my clients, I often invoke one of my favorite quotes from Eleanor Roosevelt because it's so on point: "Happiness is not a goal...it's a by-product of a life well lived." That brilliant lady knew what she was talking about! Happiness doesn't materialize when you view it as the objective. It's really a bonus from doing the work.

Why? How come continuous happiness can't be the goal? I'll tell you why: because it won't be effective. Actually, if you're focused solely on happiness as an outcome, it can even get in the way.

Let's unpack this one.

Whistle While You Work

As odd as it sounds, needing to be "happy" can feel like a burden. That's because being happy all the time is not sustainable in the real world. And what are we looking for in our goals? Doability. And what are we looking for in our success? Sustainability.

So, *trying* to be happy all the time is counterproductive. We're people. Human beings. Like it or not, we're going to feel all the feelings. If we come up against a challenge or setback, we're likely to feel worried or disappointed. If we have a conflict at work or in our relationship, why wouldn't we feel a bit anxious or frustrated? If we hit some stormy weather during our adventures, we may feel discouraged, seeking shelter and shifting our plans.

Even after reading this book and following its tenets, will you be a high achiever who feels happy every moment of every single day?

No. That's not anyone's truth. And it's therefore not helpful to chase. Striving to be or expecting to be happy every moment will not serve you. In fact, according to a recent study in the *Journal of Positive Psychology*, "Research has found that placing a high value on experiencing moment-to-moment happiness leads to negative well-being outcomes, whereas prioritizing happiness promoting behaviors has the opposite effect."[1] "Behaviors" is the operative word.

In other words, if we expect to feel happy all the time, we'll be disappointed—with ourselves and with the world. As we've established, rejecting negative emotions—hoping to experience none—is not a realistic way of living and therefore can only make you feel like you're failing. These same researchers explained that a decline in well-being was linked to a "pressure to feel happy at all times, paradoxically decreasing positive emotion."[2] So hold off on that smiley-face emoji until you legitimately need it! Otherwise, simply experiencing your natural negative emotions, especially in the face of obstacles and swamps, will begin to make you feel like you're unable to meet the "happiness goal." Remember: No one is happy all the time, no matter what those filtered and posed Instagram photos may suggest. And expecting otherwise is not allowing for the variability of each day and even moment. It makes being human seem like a flaw. And that can lead to feeling distressed, defeated, and inadequate.

Keep Those 8 Essentials in Your Rucksack

So, what does this mean for you? It means that forcing happiness is not going to bring you more joy. But doing the work—the work we've learned to do here together—can. After all, while chasing constant happiness equals unhappiness, practicing positive *behaviors* increases joy in the long term. This gives you a concrete place to constructively channel your energy!

The first challenge is to catch yourself when you're going off course. You're a pro at this. Maybe you notice some deviations in your sleep schedule? Some unhealthy food choices? The most important thing is to catch the slip. Then ask yourself: How can I rock the 8 Essentials right now?

First stop: a rest area for weary travelers—self-care central. (The explorer metaphor just keeps on giving!) That could mean something small like squeezing the stress ball on your desk and deep breathing for a minute—Maui, anyone? Or simply shutting off your phone, going to bed early, and getting some solid sleep.

Ask yourself: How can I invest in my S.E.L.F.-care right now? What physical activity can I do—maybe a walk between meetings to feel refreshed and recharged? What is one fun, relaxing, or pleasant activity I can look forward to doing today or this week? Can I get outside and enjoy nature for even a few minutes?

What is one action you can do to show support and regard for yourself today? Can you connect with someone who makes you feel seen and encouraged? Can you help someone else or practice some gratitude (break out that journal or text a heartfelt thank-you)? What is a victory you can take the time to celebrate, reminding yourself of your strengths and abilities?

Once you've implemented some helpful behaviors, clue in to your thoughts or what you're telling yourself. For example, I encourage you to strategically shift your focus from "How can I be happy right now?" to "How can I live well right now? How can I create an excellent life as I live my way into the future?"

Think back to the Excellence Equation. Honor each of the three elements: Happy (mind), Healthy (body), and High-Achieving (spirit).

Start working with the Essentials, every day. Watch out for the Troublesome Trifecta. For instance, perhaps you'll find yourself worrying, "What if I'm never a happy high achiever?" Try shifting that to: "How can I optimize my self-talk in this moment? Are there any cognitive distortions in which I can poke holes?"

Stay curious about what's driving your unhelpful thought. Maybe you're assuming others are happier than you or progressing faster in their careers. (Stop scrolling on social media!) Maybe you've decided you *should* be further along in life. Maybe you're fixating on *everything* you still want to achieve rather than remembering how much you've already done and what you can be grateful for in your life right now.

Catch those distortions! Poke holes in them. Conquer them. And then keep working the tools.

Do the work! You don't need to do everything perfectly or all of them all at once. The key is to simply use some portion of your tools *consistently* and in *combination* with one another to keep your skills sharp and the Essentials working for you. If it feels overwhelming to think about all 8, just pick one this week that you're really going to work on. Because optimizing your behaviors and thoughts in even one or two of these ways each day will set you up for success. And *yes*, even happiness.

BE KIND TO YOURSELF WHILE YOU DO THE WORK

We both know you're going to try your hardest to practice the Essentials. After all, you're an achiever by nature! And yet sometimes… you're liable to stumble or lose momentum.

Remember how we talked about patting yourself on the back for catching unbalanced thoughts instead of reprimanding yourself for falling into a cognitive distortion? Well, you can apply that same concept when you slip into unhealthy patterns.

Previously, when we discussed the concept of EAO in Essential #5, we touched on the importance of practicing empathy—how it can be helpful to treat yourself as you would a dear friend and avoid harsh self-judgment. That still stands, but now, as you work to maintain and build on what you're creating for yourself, we're taking it up a notch: While empathy is about understanding a person's feelings, compassion is the desire to help lessen a person's suffering.[3] It's the *essential* (ahem) companion for empathy.

Self-Compassion Is for Real

When I mention "self-compassion" to my patients, my words are often met with perfunctory nods or even scrunched-up noses. In other words, my clients balk. To many, this feels like some woo-woo New Age stuff without a truly solid foundation.

"Isn't self-compassion," they wonder, "for the weak, the self-indulgent, the unmotivated, the soft?"

In fact, nothing could be further from the truth. Self-compassion is a solid, legitimate, science-backed tool for productivity and reaching potential. It is directly linked to resilience and success. "Research... has shown that self-compassion makes a person more resilient, more able to bounce back," write Rick Hanson, PhD, and his son Forrest Hanson in their book *Resilient*. "It lowers self-criticism and builds up self-worth, helping you to be more ambitious and successful, not complacent and lazy."[4] Self-compassion keeps us from getting stuck in shoulds, for one thing. It also keeps us from wasting precious energy beating ourselves up and tearing ourselves down.

There are concrete benefits to exercising this approach, especially reciprocally. "Giving compassion lowers stress and calms your body," continue the authors. "Receiving compassion makes you stronger: more able to take a breath, find your footing, and keep on going. You get the benefits of both giving and receiving compassion when you offer it to yourself."[5] So maybe you don't need to run for cover at the utterance of the term "self-compassion." Maybe—just maybe—it's key to your success!

Slip and Slide

In fact, self-compassion is more important now than ever. Because on your path to finding balance and operating in excellence using the 8 Essentials, there will be slipups. We know this. After all, we've established that perfection isn't a realistic or maintainable goal.

The truth is that everyone will fail or falter, make mistakes or missteps, or make less-than-ideal choices—especially people striving to achieve big goals throughout their lifetime. There will be times when you fall into familiar traps—for instance, thinking you're not good enough, comparing yourself with others, neglecting your self-care. And in these moments, if we want to be the ones who can get up again and again in the face of adversity and charge toward our goals, we have to find compassion for ourselves.

You don't have to like making mistakes, but beating yourself up for being human doesn't help anyone. The error doesn't have to mean anything about you as a *person*. That's what's going to allow you to stand back up and spelunk another day, implementing your tools. And standing back up may be the single most important factor if you want to continually make progress in your life. "By caring and expressing concern for yourself during hard times, you're able to persevere and create changes," writes journalist Cassie Shortsleeve in her *Women's Health* article "How to Practice Self-Compassion and Build a Stable Sense of Confidence." "When you can sit with your pain and think through what you might need to achieve your goal—like waking up earlier for runs or scheduling them on your phone calendar—instead of spiraling over all the ways you're failing, you'll overcome challenges, building confidence and belief in yourself as you go."[6]

To be a lifelong sustainable high achiever, it's crucial that you help yourself in hard moments so you keep moving forward. Don't kick yourself while you're down. It'll only keep you down longer. Learn. Problem-solve. Offer yourself both understanding and kindness. Pick yourself up and keep doing the work to achieve your meaningful goals. Because self-compassion isn't about cavalierly letting yourself off the hook or not taking responsibility for your actions. It's a powerful survival skill that helps lessen your suffering and keeps you energized, even when you've taken a wrong turn or stumbled into rough terrain.

So the next time you make a mistake or don't meet a goal or drop your Essentials for a minute, instead of pouring salt in your wound, throw some self-compassion your way. Give yourself a hand and stand yourself back up.

Remind yourself that growing pains are a natural part of life—and the process of becoming your best self. As Maya Angelou said, "We delight in the beauty of the butterfly, but rarely admit the changes it has gone through to achieve that beauty."[7]

How to Exercise Self-Compassion When You Backslide

Of course, as with many ingrained habits, the idea of adopting self-compassion can seem challenging to achievers who are accustomed to berating themselves. Learning compassion can seem daunting. But it can be done! "Research shows not only that we can learn to be more self-compassionate," writes expert researcher on the topic Kristin Neff, PhD, in her book *Fierce Self-Compassion*, "but that it radically changes our lives for the better."[8]

But how?

First step: gentler self-talk. "The motivational core of self-compassion is kindness," adds Dr. Neff. "Even people who are unfailingly kind to others often treat themselves like crap. Self-kindness reverses this tendency so that we are genuinely good to ourselves. When we recognize we've made a mistake, self-kindness means that we're understanding and accepting, encouraging ourselves to do better next time."[9]

It's a Bird, It's a Plane... It's a Self-Talk Superhero!

Gentler self-talk means encouraging instead of criticizing ourselves, even in the face of slipups or when we forget to use our Essentials and perpetuate less helpful habits.

And that's what you'll need to maintain on your journey as a happier high achiever. You will make mistakes. But helpful self-talk and seizing the moment with forward-moving action is what will get you through. Again, it's not the failures that will determine your success; it will be your ability to get yourself back up on the proverbial horse and keep on riding your way to achieving your meaningful goals. This is how you build your legacy.

Indeed, what you tell yourself after a slip is what will determine your trajectory. So when the project fails, you don't earn the A or get the promotion, or your self-care becomes less than stellar and you start to should yourself, let healthy self-talk rescue you. Be kind to yourself! Become your own self-talk superhero. Up, up, and away!

From that vantage point, you can coach yourself through your missteps and setbacks. Encourage yourself with truth-based, hope-inducing statements:

> *I wish that hadn't happened, but I got this.*
> *One mistake doesn't mean defeat.*
> *I can learn from this and figure out what to do differently next time.*

Think how much better you would feel focusing on those balanced thoughts versus thinking: "Wow, I really screwed up. There's no coming back from this. I suck."

Use your self-talk to practice self-compassion and lift yourself up after a slip. Then as soon as possible, take action. Just do something healthy. Take a positive step forward. I'm talking microstep. The smallest, most doable, present-moment action—to make progress toward one of your goals and honor what you want for yourself. And use the lessons you learned from the times you lost or failed to help you create new wins that motivate you. It will rebuild your momentum and prevent slip-induced inertia. It will keep you from getting stuck.

Your reward for practicing self-compassion, resetting, and starting again? Resilience, confidence, and progress.

LOVE THE WORK...
'CAUSE THE WORK IS YOUR LIFE!

When we talk about doing the work of putting these 8 Essentials into practice, no doubt it initially seems challenging. After all, you're a high achiever and, as we've established, adding something else to your to-do list can sound exhausting. But what we've been discussing here isn't about sapping your energy. It's about living your best life. It's about fueling your vigor. It's about using your energy in healthy, meaningful ways that will actually, ultimately, *keep* you energized. So use your energy! Because that's what will allow it to regenerate and keep working for you.

After all, you will never reach excellence and be done. You will have many wins and successes with the 8 Essentials, but you will continually work with them as you and your circumstances grow and change. These are meant to be lifelong guiding practices to bolster you throughout the years.

That means finding joy in the process—not just awaiting joy in the outcome. It means looking for comfort in the tools because you can return to them again and again for solace. These are the constants as you navigate the challenges of life. It means celebrating the small victories along the way, even if that simply means that you successfully poked holes in a distorted thought. It means looking for color in what might otherwise seem like a dull palette. "In a boring afternoon meeting, finding something, anything, to enjoy about it will keep you awake and make you more effective," says *Resilient* author Rick Hanson, PhD. And, he notes, "Enjoying life is a powerful way to care for yourself."[10]

Simply by choosing to shine your flashlight on the elements of the process that are pleasurable, fascinating, or informative, you actually increase your chance of feeling better, decreasing your worry and distress. Though the notion of "enjoying the process" or "making the journey the destination" has become somewhat pat, there is real truth in its core concept. And this goes back to the pursuit of excellence over perfection. If you are living your life in pursuit of doing your best, then you get to enjoy the fruits of knowing you tried hard and left nothing on the table. And you can feel at peace with that.

In her book *Mindset: How We Can Learn to Fulfill Our Potential*, Carol S. Dweck, PhD, details some of the most renowned athletes and found they had a "growth mindset" in common. In other words, the joy was not just in winning but rather in knowing that they had improved or done their best. "I derive just as much happiness from the process as from the results," said legendary track-and-field athlete Jackie Joyner-Kersee. "If I lose, I just go back to the track and work some more."[11] Ultimately, Dr. Dweck found that people with this outlook, winners who prioritized growth, found setbacks motivating instead of defeating.

Not every moment is going to be fun. Patterns involving anxiety, burnout, and imposter syndrome don't go away overnight. It takes time to heal. But if you can congratulate yourself when you notice yourself improving, if you can value learning from mistakes rather than fear them, and if you can enjoy the new self-care regimen that makes you function so much more optimally, then you can get the most out of your life.

For me, my daily work offers a lot of joy. I am grateful for it. I love helping people and I relish rooting for my clients to succeed. It feels awesome to help my patients achieve their goals! But of course, there are elements I find a bit less engaging. When my job involves a lot of paperwork and documentation instead of human interaction, for example, sometimes I find myself less enthralled. I, too, use self-talk to help myself find and remember the enjoyment in it. I tell myself that the clinical notes are necessary and useful. I remind myself that I feel like the best version of myself when I get to sit in my chair as Dr. A. I'm truly fortunate. And that gratitude helps me stay focused on the meaning in my work. Similarly, it's not always easy to make time to work out, but once I'm on the treadmill I enjoy my upbeat tunes and how strong my body feels when it's moving.

In these ways, we can enjoy what might otherwise feel like drudgery or hard work. Not that we're going to adore every minute. But that there are grains of joy to be found along the way.

Ultimately, this book is a touchstone for you. The more accustomed you get to implementing the 8 Essentials, the more automatically you'll put them into effect. And your path to excellence can only expand with these tools. This is what it means to be a happy high achiever. It's reaching your meaningful goals with enthusiasm, confidence, and a sense of purpose beyond pleasing others. It's making your mark, leaving your legacy, and feeling proud and inspired by your own achievement!

I created these guiding principles because they're sustainable—because they allow you to live optimally, to access more of what makes you *you*, and to achieve in ways you never imagined. So continue to use the practices. Find your success. Pursue your excellence again and again. Learn to refuel and manage your energy such that you can make all of your amazing talents, power, and proclivities of high achievement work for you throughout your lifetime.

YOUR 8 ESSENTIALS TO-GO

I defy the tyranny of precedent. I go for anything new that might improve the past.

—Clara Barton

Way back at the beginning of this book, I introduced my client Agnes, who in a moment of utter anxiety and overwhelm asked me, "How do I get through the rest of my day?"

Remember her? I know I do. Those words echoed in my head for years afterward.

And in many ways, that's the question this book is built to answer.

For Agnes, like so many of my other high achievers, the answer lay in helping her be more of her authentic self. That meant working the 8 Essentials to stop people-pleasing and lessen the immense career pressure she felt by setting boundaries and listening to her own instincts. It meant figuring out what *she* valued, instead of seeking approval and validation from others, and minimizing social comparison. No longer bogged down by self-doubt, she soared at work.

One important act of self-care for her outside the office was to incorporate a beloved hobby back into her life, signing up for a figure drawing class. That served as both an outlet to release stress and also something to look forward to each week. Still, Agnes needed to remind herself again and again to be her own self-talk superhero. To help, she framed that *excellent* William James quote: "The greatest weapon against stress is our ability to choose one thought over another." I wouldn't be surprised if it still sits on her desk to this day.

Of course, our sessions eventually came to an end. With a full and proud heart, I stood up from my chair, set my notes down, wished her well, and said goodbye. She waved as she headed out but then turned back to face me in the doorway. "One more thing, Dr. A," she said as I looked up. "Thank you for helping me feel better—and more... myself."

That's it! That's the goal. That's why I do this. I can't tell you how elated it makes me when my patients do the work and get to see that the work *works*.

She did it. Like so many others before. She went from struggling with anxiety to finding relief—and then, ultimately, feeling joy. Agnes transformed her life for the better. And you can, too.

So how do you get through the day? When things are tough. When you feel insecure, paralyzed by perfectionism, worn out. When the swamp gets particularly murky. By mirroring what Agnes did: Using the 8 Essentials, she changed what thoughts she chose to focus on and found doable ways to make healthy habits a part of her everyday life. She accepted, honored, and even was grateful for who she is today and all she hopes to become. While the exact details vary, the reality is that, for all of my brilliant and anxious high achievers, the key to sustainable success—achievement without crippling anxiety, self-doubt, and exhaustion—is working with these principles, again and again.

I know that's not always easy. It's one thing to practice these tools while moving your way through this book or in your apartment without the noise of the outside world to interrupt. It's another to mindfully bring them into daily practice each day as you navigate a complicated landscape.

That's why, in my final session with patients, we review what I call the quantum leaps of progress they've made throughout therapy and help them create a therapy takeaways list of what they learned throughout our time together. We discuss what strategies and messages were most meaningful to them. It's always fascinating what resonates most—and really stays with them. I hand-write the list, bullet-pointing each noteworthy nugget, then peel the sheet of lined paper from my pad and hand it over.

Well, I can't hand you a slip of paper. But I'm not going to let that stop me! Below I've created a kind of *CliffsNotes* version for you—your 8 Essentials To-Go.

Snap a picture! Keep it on your phone. (New screensaver, anyone?) Reference it often. Let this list be a touchstone as you move through your life, navigating swamps, celebrating small and large victories, setting and meeting meaningful goals. Let this list help you find your brightest future. Let it lead you to be your most excellent you.

---

8 ESSENTIALS TO-GO

ESSENTIAL # 1:
STRIVE FOR EXCELLENCE, NOT PERFECTION

Perfectionism is the Achilles' heel of the ambitious. Excellence allows space for high achievement—and your humanity!

ESSENTIAL # 2:
INVEST IN THE ULTIMATE CURRENCY: YOUR ENERGY

Self-care is not self-indulgent—it's necessary and strategic. Calendar it. Embrace wiggle room. Rock the S.E.L.F.-care fundamentals to beat burnout and enjoy high performance.

ESSENTIAL # 3:
NAVIGATE UNCERTAINTY WITH CURIOSITY

Worry is thinking about the future with fear. Wonder is thinking about the future with curiosity. Instead of Jumping to Conclusions, turn Worry to Wonder—and Stay Curious.

ESSENTIAL # 4:
CULTIVATE HEALTHY CONNECTIONS

Excellence is a collaborative endeavor. Set kind, assertive boundaries. Find your Easy People! Ask yourself: How does this person impact my energy and stress levels?

ESSENTIAL # 5:
TRANSFORM *SHOULDS* TO *CANS*

Shoulds—whether directed at ourselves, others, or situations—keep us stuck. We all have our turn in the swamp. Awareness, acceptance, and action move us forward.

ESSENTIAL # 6:
LEVEL UP TO GRATITUDE-BASED THINKING

GRATITUDE ➡ HAPPINESS ➡ SUCCESS—not the other way around! Triumph over the whole Troublesome Trifecta with a thank-you!

ESSENTIAL # 7:
CELEBRATE THE VICTORIES

Use your memories of past successes as fuel as you climb your next mountain. Pause to rejoice in the good. Play! Fun can move you forward.

ESSENTIAL # 8:
CURATE MEANINGFUL GOALS, CREATE YOUR LEGACY– START NOW!

Hop off the conveyor belt and choose meaningful goals. Purpose is what will help you persevere and feel proud. Full steam ahead to sustainable success!

Look, here's what I want to tell you above all else, as we get ready to part ways: It's going to take time to make big goals and dreams come true. You are poised for excellence, and knowing your *why* is what will keep you going. These days, people often tell you to be your best self. Every other Instagram post professes some version of that phrase! And yet people rarely tell you why. Why strive to be your best?

It's not to prove anything. Definitely not. You don't need to strive for anyone else's sake. Or to be someone other than who you are. The reason to strive is so you can live with the most happiness, ease, and excellence. Because when you are striving to be your best, the way *you* define it, that's when you will *feel* your best—which you deserve.

Thanks to the powerful relationship between thoughts, feelings, and behaviors, when you implement your best self-talk and self-care, you will feel good. You don't have to ride to the brink of burnout to be high-achieving. You can shine brightly and share your most excellent self from an energized, joy-filled, purpose-driven place. That will make you the most motivated, productive, and *successful*. And that's when you'll show up in the world as your best, which will benefit you and others.

• • •

I believe we are made for joy. So if this book can be a resource for hope, comfort, and inspiration; if it can keep you on track to your excellent summits; if it can help you be more of who you are—someone incredible and worthy, fully you—I will have succeeded in my own meaningful goal. I hope you'll come back to it when you need a refresher, an encouraging word, a motivating boost.

You are never alone. I believe in you. And there are so many people, countless companions around the world, on parallel journeys to transform from anxious to happy high achievers. By reading this book, you've already started working to feel better. To approach rather than avoid your fears. And my hope is you've discovered this truth, as Agnes did: Accept and be who you truly are—and you won't feel as anxious. Yep, when you accept your imperfect-but-valuable-as-you-are self, you'll spend less time worrying about what other people think of you, about expectations of how you "should" be or what activities you "should" enjoy. You won't waste your time and energy. Instead, you'll do things you actually find meaningful. You'll give the world *you*. And that's awesome.

Now keep the momentum going. Stay aware of your self-talk. Refocus your flashlight as necessary. The choice of where to shine your light is in your hands.

You can overcome your anxiety. You can create and maintain excellent habits. You can persevere through mistakes or difficult moments and keep moving forward. You can be a happy, healthy high achiever and enjoy an excellent life. And you will leave an indelible mark upon the world in a unique way that only you can.

Your mark matters.

Now go—you got this!

ACKNOWLEDGMENTS

I am grateful to so many people for helping me bring this book to life and share it with the world. I've truly felt like Dorothy on my own amazing Yellow Brick Road—accompanied and assisted by numerous fantastic people so I could arrive here today. I am excited, proud, and thankful to now celebrate with you all!

First, my sincere gratitude to Dr. Rick Hanson. Your tremendously encouraging words and generosity of spirit at our serendipitous meeting in San Diego at a conference several years ago inspired me to finally write the book I had been dreaming of—and that was the start of my journey.

Next, Kelly Notaras, I was incredibly fortunate that you were the first person to read my manuscript and enthusiastically empower me to take the next steps to transform it into the book it is today. Thank you for your instrumental guidance and thoughtful support at such an important time. You are a supremely talented, magnanimous person. I truly believe we were meant to connect.

With Kelly's help, I began working with my wonderful KN Literary marketing coach Laura Dickerson. Thank you so much, Laura! Many thanks, as well, to: Annie Wylde for your outstanding assistance with my proposal, Felicity Murphy for your phenomenal photography, and web expert extraordinaire Charlie Griffin for creating a website that I'm thrilled and honored to share. And a huge thank-you to media relations dynamo Ashley Bernardi for your masterful insights and for sending me the one-line email: "You may benefit from this! :)" that led me to *Get Signed*.

Lucinda Halpern, since I met you at that first *Get Signed* class, I knew I wanted to work with you. You are brilliant and tenacious, and most important, you have an amazing heart. I'm so grateful I met you and I'm so thankful for all of your continued expert guidance and support. This is all happening because of you. Thank you, thank you, thank you.

Thank you so much to all of the talented people who've helped me successfully navigate the publishing world: Julia Collucci, for your consistent thoughtfulness, sincerity, and assistance; Jackie Ashton, for your encouragement, guidance, and support—I'm grateful for all the time and effort you spent helping me land my book deal and for always rooting me on; Linda Sparrowe, for your invaluable assistance on this journey; everyone at Lucinda Literary for your continued help; and to Roseanne Wells, for your expertise and support in getting this book out into the world.

I'm so thankful to everyone at Hachette Book Group. Hannah Robinson, I will be forever grateful that you believed in *The Happy High Achiever* and made my childhood dream of becoming an author come true. Thank you for your tremendous kindness and brilliant insights. I'm so proud of our Team Exhilaration! Also, thank you so much to Nana Twumasi and Natalie Bautista at Balance; you've generously welcomed me and guided me through this incredible book production process. I am thrilled and grateful to be working with you.

Nora Zelevansky, I truly don't know how to thank you enough. You are an impeccable writer and a phenomenal human being. You have absolutely helped make this book the best it can be. You've been my partner in striving for excellence. It's an honor collaborating with you and a blessing to know you.

Huge thanks and hugs to my fantastic friends who were also readers for me: Dr. S. Karen Chung, Kim Gerads, Carolyn Nguyen, and Dr. Jen Wachen. I appreciate you so much, ladies!!

Thank you, Dr. Mary Henein and Dr. Xinmeng Jasmine Mu, my amazing friends in California. Our friendship over the years and our epic, inspiring phone chats mean more to me than you know.

Thank you to my awesome East Coast friends: Dr. Nicolina Calfa, Dr. Ida Kellison, Dr. Kara Naylon, Dr. Sanja Petrovic, and Katie Riley. And to Dr. Amy Bachand and the Bachand family (Michael, Aiden, and Abigail) for always making me feel like part of the family. Thank you all so much!

Thank you to everyone at LifeStance who has been so supportive of me and my book journey: Vida Rimkuviene, Dr. Marc Robert, Djurdjica Sapundzic, and all of my colleagues.

Thank you to the CPA team, including: Dr. Edouard Fontenot, Nora Harrington, Dr. Robyn Kervick, Devon Moos, Dr. Andi Piatt, Dr. Wendy Vincent, and Dave Wisholek.

Thank you to everyone at VA Boston, especially: Dr. John Otis, Dr. Keith Shaw, Dr. Amy Silberbogen, and Dr. Glenn Trezza. Also, a huge thank-you to my University of Florida graduate mentor, Dr. Michael Perri—you inspired me with your guidance to strive for excellence. I really felt that you believed in me. I can't tell you how much that meant. And thank you to Dr. Gretchen Ames, Dr. Stephen Anton, Dr. Robert Guenther, Dr. Julius Gylys, and everyone at UF who helped inspire me to be the best clinical psychologist I could be. I'll forever remember your encouragement at the start of one of our clinical days, Julius: "Let's go heal some hearts!" Yes!

Thank you to Dr. Paul Finn and Dr. Joseph Troisi and everyone at St. A's who helped me learn and love psychology.

Thank you to my teachers at Barnstable High School, especially my journalism teacher, Mr. Mick Carlon; English teacher, Mrs. Kathleen Flaherty; and psychology teacher, Mr. Mark Sullivan, for your excellent teaching and encouraging words at such a formative time in my life. And thank you to my Barnstable friends and fellow Cape Codders who've shared and contributed to my journey.

To all the people throughout my life who've inspired, encouraged, and challenged me to be the best I can be, who've helped me laugh, love, think, and keep learning and growing—I couldn't list you all here, but please know you are in my heart. Thank you, thank you, thank you.

Thank you to Julie and Mary Anne, I'm so grateful we grew up together and continue to share all of the ups and downs of life—being friends with you both since we were kids is truly a blessing.

To my big Anderson family: Bob, Beth, Samantha, Robert, Chrissy, Ian, Justin, David, Maureen, Thomas, Catie, Jim, Heather, Isabelle, Angus, Phoebe, John, Lindsay, Sophie, Chloe, all my cousins, and extended family—thank you so much for your love, support, encouragement, and so many fun moments throughout the years. I love you all.

Thank you so much, Mom, for being my hero, for always believing in me, and for inspiring me to be the kindest person I can be. To Dad, I know you are watching over all of us—and cheering me on from above. Thank you for always trying to make us smile and showing us what the magic of true love looks like every time you danced with Mom. Thank you for everything, Mom and Dad. I love you so much.

To my patients throughout the years, this book is really a thank-you letter to you. Thank you for allowing me to pull up a seat to listen to your greatest fears, worries, triumphs, and defeats. I've learned so much from accompanying you as you've worked to transform your lives for the better. I am grateful beyond words.

And to you, my dear reader, thank you so much for going on this journey with me. It's been an absolute honor and joy. With warmest regards, I wish you happiness, good health, and many excellent days ahead!

NOTES

OPTIMIZE YOUR THOUGHTS FOR SUCCESS

1. Shawn Achor, *The Happiness Advantage: How a Positive Brain Fuels Success in Work and Life* (New York: Currency, an imprint of the Crown Publishing Group, a division of Penguin Random House, 2010), 4.
2. Arlin Cuncic, "The Spotlight Effect and Social Anxiety," Verywell Mind, updated August 28, 2023, https://www.verywellmind.com/what-is-the-spotlight-effect-3024470.

UNDERSTANDING THE TROUBLESOME TRIFECTA

1. David D. Burns, *The Feeling Good Handbook*, revised edition (New York: Plume/Penguin Books, 1999).
2. Kendra Cherry, "What Is Neuroplasticity?," Verywell Mind, updated November 8, 2022, https://www.verywellmind.com/what-is-brain-plasticity-2794886.
3. Stuart Brown with Christopher Vaughan, *Play: How It Shapes the Brain, Opens the Imagination, and Invigorates the Soul* (New York: Avery, 2010), 138–41.
4. Kendra Cherry, "How Openness Affects Your Behavior," Verywell Mind, updated August 31, 2023, https://www.verywellmind.com/how-openness-influences-your-behavior-4796351.

ESSENTIAL #1: STRIVE FOR EXCELLENCE, NOT PERFECTION

1. Sharon Martin, *The CBT Workbook for Perfectionism* (Oakland, CA: New Harbinger Publications, 2019), 7.
2. Brené Brown, *The Gifts of Imperfection* (Minneapolis: Hazelden Publishing, 2010), 56–57.
3. Oprah Winfrey, "2018 USC Commencement Speech," University of Southern California Annenberg School for Journalism and Communication, May 11, 2018.

ESSENTIAL #2: INVEST IN THE ULTIMATE CURRENCY: YOUR ENERGY

1. Michael Leiter and Christina Maslach, "You Can Conquer Burnout," *Scientific American*, January 1, 2015, https://www.scientificamerican.com/article/you-can-conquer-burnout/.
2. Marily Oppezzo and Daniel L. Schwartz, "Give Your Ideas Some Legs: The Positive Effect of Walking on Creative Thinking," *Journal of Experimental Psychology: Learning, Memory, and Cognition* 40, no. 4 (April 2014): 1144.

3. May Wong, "Stanford Study Shows Walking Improves Creativity," *Stanford News*, April 24, 2014, https://news.stanford.edu/2014/04/24/walking-vs-sitting-042414/.

4. Rachel MacPherson, "6 Reasons to Take a 15 Minute Walk Today," Verywell Fit, October 2, 2023, https://www.verywellfit.com/reasons-to-take-a-15-minute-walk-7974090.

5. "More Sleep Would Make Us Happier, Healthier, and Safer," American Psychological Association, created 2014, https://www.apa.org/topics/sleep/deprivation-consequences.

6. Eric Suni and Abhinav Singh, "How Much Sleep Do You Need?," SleepFoundation.org, last updated September 8, 2023, https://www.sleepfoundation.org/how-sleep-works/how-much-sleep-do-we-really-need.

7. "10 Reasons to Get More Sleep," Healthline, last updated April 25, 2023, https://www.healthline.com/nutrition/10-reasons-why-good-sleep-is-important#The-bottom-line.

8. Gregg D. Jacobs, *Say Good Night to Insomnia*, updated edition (New York: St. Martin's Press, 2009), 90.

9. Emily Nagoski and Amelia Nagoski, *Burnout: The Secret to Unlocking the Stress Cycle* (New York: Ballantine Books, an imprint of Random House, a division of Penguin Random House, 2020), 15.

10. Mayo Clinic Staff, "Chronic Stress Puts Your Health at Risk," Mayo Clinic, August 1, 2023, https://www.mayoclinic.org/healthy-lifestyle/stress-management/in-depth/stress/art-20046037.

11. "Exercising to Relax," Harvard Health Publishing, July 7, 2020, https://www.health.harvard.edu/staying-healthy/exercising-to-relax.

12. Nagoski and Nagoski, *Burnout*, 15.

13. Mayo Clinic Staff, "Chronic Stress Puts Your Health at Risk."

14. Shawn Achor, *The Happiness Advantage: How a Positive Brain Fuels Success in Work and Life* (New York: Currency, an imprint of the Crown Publishing Group, a division of Penguin Random House, 2010), 52.

15. Ron Friedman, "What You Eat Affects Your Productivity," *Harvard Business Review*, October 17, 2014, https://hbr.org/2014/10/what-you-eat-affects-your-productivity.

16. "6 Possible Health Benefits of Deep Breathing," Everyday Health, April 10, 2023, https://www.everydayhealth.com/wellness/possible-health-benefits-of-deep-breathing/.

17. "5 Reasons Why Writing Lists Is Good for Your Mental Health," *Psychology Today*, April 19, 2023, https://www.psychologytoday.com/us/blog/when-kids-call-the-shots/202304/5-reasons-why-writing-lists-is-good-for-your-mental-health.

18. "Why Multitasking Doesn't Work," Cleveland Clinic, March 10, 2021, https://health.clevelandclinic.org/science-clear-multitasking-doesnt-work/.

19. "Should You Take an Epsom Salt Bath?," Cleveland Clinic, April 28, 2022, https://health.clevelandclinic.org/7-things-you-probably-didnt-know-about-epsom-salt/.

20. "Poor Posture Hurts Your Health More than You Realize: Tips for Fixing It," Cleveland Clinic, August 6, 2021, https://health.clevelandclinic.org/health-effects-of-poor-posture/.

21. "Stress Management: Doing Progressive Muscle Relaxation," University of Michigan Health, accessed December 7, 2021, https://www.uofmhealth.org./health-library/uz2225.

22. "Is Laughter Good for Lung Health?," American Lung Association, last updated August 21, 2023, https://www.lung.org/blog/laughter-for-lungs.

23. Sheryl Ankrom, "9 Deep Breathing Exercises to Reduce Anxiety," Verywell Mind, last updated January 27, 2023, https://www.verywellmind.com/abdominal-breathing-2584115.

24. Jim Sollisch, "The Cure for Decision Fatigue," *Wall Street Journal*, June 10, 2016, https://www.wsj.com/articles/the-cure-for-decision-fatigue-1465596928.

25. Grant A. Pignatiello, Richard J. Martin, and Ronald L. Hickman Jr., "Decision Fatigue: A Conceptual Analysis," *Journal of Health Psychology* 25, no. 1 (March 2018), https://doi.org/10.1177/1359105318763510.

26. John Tierney, "Do You Suffer From Decision Fatigue?," *New York Times*, August 17, 2011, https://www.nytimes.com/2011/08/21/magazine/do-you-suffer-from-decision-fatigue.html?smid=nytcore-ios-share&referringSource=articleShare.

27. Sara Berg, "What Doctors Wish Patients Knew About Decision Fatigue," American Medical Association, November 19, 2021, https://www.ama-assn.org/delivering-care/public-health/what-doctors-wish-patients-knew-about-decision-fatigue.

28. Emma Seppala, "Why You Should Take More Time Off from Work," *Greater Good Magazine*, August 10, 2017, https://greatergood.berkeley.edu/article/item/why_you_should_take_more_time_off_from_work.

29. Rebecca Zucker, "How Taking a Vacation Improves Your Well-Being," *Harvard Business Review*, July 19, 2023, https://hbr.org/2023/07/how-taking-a-vacation-improves-your-well-being.

ESSENTIAL #3: NAVIGATE UNCERTAINTY WITH CURIOSITY

1. Rick Hanson, *Hardwiring Happiness* (New York: Harmony Books, 2013), 20.

2. *Concise Oxford English Dictionary*, twelfth edition (New York: Oxford University Press, 2011), 351.

3. Tracy Brower, "The Future Is Uncertain: 5 Ways to Embrace Ambiguity," *Forbes*, January 10, 2022, https://www.forbes.com/sites/tracybrower/2022/01/10/the-future-is-uncertain-5-ways-to-embrace-ambiguity/?sh=13d658001c2c.

ESSENTIAL #4: CULTIVATE HEALTHY CONNECTIONS

1. John D. Otis, *Managing Chronic Pain: A Cognitive Behavioral Therapy Approach* (New York: Oxford University Press, 2007), 45–50.

2. Ann Pietrangelo, "What the Yerkes-Dodson Law Says About Stress and Performance," *Healthline*, October 22, 2020, https://www.healthline.com/health/yerkes-dodson-law.

3. Seth J. Gillihan, *Cognitive Behavioral Therapy Made Simple* (Emeryville, CA: Althea Press, 2018), 22.

4. Brooke C. Feeney and Nancy L. Collins, "A New Look at Social Support: A Theoretical Perspective on Thriving Through Relationships," *Personality and Social Psychology Review* 19, no. 2 (May 2015): 113–47, https://doi.org/10.1177/1088868314544.

5. "Press Release: Social Support: Carnegie Mellon's Brooke Feeney Details How to Thrive Through Close Relationships," Carnegie Mellon University website, September 5, 2014, https://www.cmu.edu/news/stories/archives/2014/september/september5_feeneyrelationshipsupport.html.

6. Fatih Ozbay, Douglas C. Johnson, Eleni Dimoulas, C. A. Morgan III, Dennis Charney, and Steven Southwick, "Social Support and Resilience to Stress," *Psychiatry (Edgmont)* 4 (May 2007): 35–40, https://www.ncbi.nlm.nih.gov/pmc/articles/PMC2921311/.

7. Robert Waldinger, "What Makes a Good Life? Lessons from the Longest Study on Happiness," TED Talk, November 2015, https://www.ted.com/talks/robert_waldinger_what_makes_a_good_life_lessons_from_the_longest_study_on_happiness.

8. Vivek H. Murthy, "Letter from the Surgeon General," *Our Epidemic of Loneliness and Isolation 2023: The US Surgeon General's Advisory on the Healing Effects of Social Connection and Community* (May 2023): 4–5.

9. Sigal Barsade and Hakan Ozcelik, "The Painful Cycle of Employee Loneliness and How It Hurts Companies," *Harvard Business Review*, April 24, 2018, https://hbr.org/2018/04/the-painful-cycle-of-employee-loneliness-and-how-it-hurts-companies.

10. Hakan Ozcelik and Sigal G. Barsade, "No Employee an Island: Workplace Loneliness and Job Performance," *Academy of Management Journal* 61, no. 6 (December 2018): 2344–66, https://doi.org/10.5465/amj.2015.1066.

11. Barbara Fredrickson, *Love 2.0: How Our Supreme Emotion Affects Everything We Think, Do, Feel, and Become* (New York: Avery, 2013), 17.

12. Larry Dossey, "The Helper's High," *Explore* 14, no. 6 (November 2018): 393–99, https://www.sciencedirect.com/science/article/pii/S1550830718304178?via%3Dihub.

13. "Why Giving Is Good for Your Health," Cleveland Clinic, December 7, 2022, https://health.clevelandclinic.org/why-giving-is-good-for-your-health/.

14. Sherrie Bourg Carter, "Helper's High: The Benefits (and Risks) of Altruism," PsychologyToday.com, September 4, 2014, https://www.psychologytoday.com/us/blog/high-octane-women/201409/helpers-high-the-benefits-and-risks-altruism.

15. Kurt Vonnegut, *Palm Sunday* (New York: Dial Press Trade Paperbacks, an imprint of the Random House Publishing Group, 2011), 293.

16. Sharon Martin, *The CBT Workbook for Perfectionism* (Oakland, CA: New Harbinger Publications, 2019), 131.

17. Martin, *The CBT Workbook for Perfectionism*.

18. John D. Otis, *Managing Chronic Pain: A Cognitive-Behavioral Therapy Approach Workbook* (New York: Oxford University Press, 2007), 69.

ESSENTIAL #5: TRANSFORM *SHOULDS* TO *CANS*

1. Sharon Martin, *The CBT Workbook for Perfectionism* (Oakland, CA: New Harbinger Publications, 2019), 68.
2. K. Blaine Lawlor and Martin J. Hornyak, "Smart Goals: How the Application of Smart Goals Can Contribute to Achievement of Student Learning Outcomes," *Developments in Business Simulation and Experiential Learning* 39 (April 2012): 259–67, https://absel-ojs-ttu.tdl.org/absel/index.php/absel/article/view/90.
3. "Dark Chocolate Health Benefits," Cleveland Clinic, March 10, 2022, https://health.clevelandclinic.org/dark-chocolate-health-benefits/.
4. Martin, *The CBT Workbook for Perfectionism*, 162.
5. Carl R. Rogers, *A Way of Being* (New York: HarperCollins Publishers, 1980), 22.
6. Julie Corliss, "Want to Feel More Connected? Practice Empathy," Harvard Health Publishing, February 22, 2021, https://www.health.harvard.edu/blog/want-to-feel-more-connected-practice-empathy-2021022221992.
7. Viktor E. Frankl, *Man's Search for Meaning* (Boston: Beacon Press, 2006), 66 (first published 1959 by Beacon Press).

ESSENTIAL #6: LEVEL UP TO GRATITUDE-BASED THINKING

1. Robert A. Emmons, *The Little Book of Gratitude* (London: Gaia, 2016), 9.
2. Brené Brown, *Atlas of the Heart* (New York: Random House, 2021), 214.
3. Courtney E. Ackerman, "28 Benefits of Gratitude & Most Significant Research Findings," PositivePsychology.com, October 9, 2021, https://positivepsychology.com/benefits-gratitude-research-questions/.
4. Robert A. Emmons, *Gratitude Works!: A 21-Day Program for Creating Emotional Prosperity* (San Francisco: Jossey-Bass, A Wiley Imprint, 2013), 10.
5. David Steindl-Rast, "Want to Be Happy? Be Grateful," TED Talk, June 2013, 14:17, https://www.ted.com/talks/david_steindl_rast_want_to_be_happy_be_grateful?.
6. Shawn Achor, *The Happiness Advantage: How a Positive Brain Fuels Success in Work and Life* (New York: Currency, an imprint of the Crown Publishing Group, a division of Penguin Random House, 2010), 4.
7. Steindl-Rast, "Want to Be Happy? Be Grateful."
8. Richard G. Tedeschi and Lawrence G. Calhoun, "Posttraumatic Growth: Conceptual Foundations and Empirical Evidence," *Psychological Inquiry* 15, no. 1 (2004): 1–18.
9. Scott Barry Kaufman, "Post-Traumatic Growth: Finding Meaning and Creativity in Adversity," *Scientific American*, April 20, 2020, https://blogs.scientificamerican.com/beautiful-minds/post-traumatic-growth-finding-meaning-and-creativity-in-adversity/.
10. Kaufman, "Post-Traumatic Growth: Finding Meaning and Creativity in Adversity."
11. Tal Ben-Shahar, *Happiness Studies: An Introduction* (Cham, Switzerland: Palgrave Macmillan, an imprint of Springer Nature Switzerland, 2021), 112.

12. John D. Otis, *Managing Chronic Pain: A Cognitive Behavioral Therapy Approach* (New York: Oxford University Press, 2007), 26–28.
13. "How Guided Imagery Helps You Relax," Cleveland Clinic, February 28, 2022, https://health.clevelandclinic.org/guided-imagery/.
14. Haruki Murakami, *Kafka on the Shore* (New York: Vintage, an Imprint of Random House, 2005).

ESSENTIAL #7: CELEBRATE THE VICTORIES

1. Rick Hanson, *Hardwiring Happiness* (New York: Harmony Books, 2013), 27.
2. Hanson, *Hardwiring Happiness*, 31.
3. Whitney Johnson, "Celebrate to Win," *Harvard Business Review*, January 26, 2022, https://hbr.org/2022/01/celebrate-to-win.
4. Hanson, *Hardwiring Happiness*, 28.
5. Hanson, *Hardwiring Happiness*.
6. Brad Stulberg and Steve Magness, *Peak Performance* (New York: Rodale Books, 2017), 113–15.
7. Johnson, "Celebrate to Win."
8. Benjamin Cheyette and Sarah Cheyette, "Why It's Important to Celebrate Small Successes," *Psychology Today*, November 22, 2021, https://www.psychologytoday.com/us/blog/1-2-3-adhd/202111/why-its-important-celebrate-small-successes.
9. John C. Maxwell, *How Successful People Think* (New York: Center Street, 2009), 71.
10. Stuart Brown with Christopher Vaughan, *Play: How It Shapes the Brain, Opens the Imagination, and Invigorates the Soul* (New York: Avery, 2010), 110–11.
11. Kirsten Weir, "Nurtured by Nature," *Monitor on Psychology* 51, no. 3 (April 1, 2020): 50.
12. Cheyette and Cheyette, "Why It's Important to Celebrate Small Successes."
13. Johnson, "Celebrate to Win."

ESSENTIAL #8: CURATE MEANINGFUL GOALS, CREATE YOUR LEGACY—START NOW!

1. Viktor E. Frankl, *Man's Search for Meaning* (Boston: Beacon Press, 2006), 105 (first published 1959 by Beacon Press).
2. Kimberly Wade-Benzoni, "How to Think About Building Your Legacy," *Harvard Business Review*, December 15, 2016, https://hbr.org/2016/12/how-to-think-about-building-your-legacy.
3. Colin Schultz, "Blame Sloppy Journalism for the Nobel Prizes," *Smithsonian Magazine*, October 9, 2013, https://www.smithsonianmag.com/smart-news/blame-sloppy-journalism-for-the-nobel-prizes-1172688/.
4. "Who We Are and What We Do," Nobel Prize Organisation, accessed November 26, 2021, https://www.nobelprize.org/the-nobel-prize-organisation/.
5. Steve Jobs, "Commencement Address," Stanford University, June 12, 2005, 15:04, https://news.stanford.edu/2005/06/14/jobs-061505/.

6. Kurt Vonnegut, *Palm Sunday* (New York: Dial Press Trade Paperbacks, an imprint of the Random House Publishing Group, 2011), 293.

ENJOYING A LIFETIME OF EXCELLENCE

1. Ashley Humphrey, Rebecca Szoka, and Brock Bastian, "When the Pursuit of Happiness Backfires," *The Journal of Positive Psychology* 17, no. 5 (March 2021): 611–19, https://doi.org/10.1080/17439760.2021.1897869.
2. Humphrey, Szoka, and Bastian, "When the Pursuit of Happiness Backfires."
3. Kendra Cherry, "Compassion vs. Empathy: What's the Difference?," Verywell Mind, updated June 5, 2023, https://www.verywellmind.com/compassion-vs-empathy-what-s-the-difference-7494906.
4. Rick Hanson, with Forrest Hanson, *Resilient* (New York: Harmony Books, 2018), 14.
5. Hanson and Hanson, *Resilient*.
6. Cassie Shortsleeve, "How to Practice Self-Compassion and Build a Stable Sense of Confidence," *Women's Health*, December 30, 2022, https://www.womenshealthmag.com/health/a42156653/self-compassion-how-to-be-more-confident/.
7. Maya Angelou, *Rainbow in the Cloud: The Wisdom and Spirit of Maya Angelou* (New York: Random House, 2014), 97.
8. Kristin Neff, *Fierce Self-Compassion* (New York: HarperWave, an imprint of HarperCollins, 2021), 11.
9. Neff, *Fierce Self-Compassion*, 23.
10. Hanson and Hanson, *Resilient*, 19–20.
11. Carol S. Dweck, *Mindset: How We Can Learn to Fulfill Our Potential* (New York: Ballantine Books, 2006), 98.

ABOUT THE AUTHOR

Dr. Mary Anderson is a licensed psychologist and sought-after speaker with over a decade of experience helping patients become happier, healthier, and sustainably high-achieving. Dr. Anderson earned her PhD in clinical psychology, with a specialty in health psychology, from the University of Florida and completed her internship and post doctoral fellowship at the VA Boston Healthcare System, with appointments at Harvard Medical School and Boston University School of Medicine. She currently lives in Boston, Massachusetts.